# KYOTO

## Seven Paths to the Heart of the City

Diane Durston

KODANSHA INTERNATIONAL
Tokyo and New York

Distributed in the United States by Kodansha International/USA
Ltd., through Harper & Row, Publishers, Inc., 10 East 53rd Street,
New York, New York 10022.

Published by Kodansha International Ltd., 2-2, Otowa 1-chome,
Bunkyo-ku, Tokyo 112 and Kodansha International/USA Ltd.,
10 East 53rd Street, New York, New York 10022, in cooperation
with Mitsumura Suiko Shoin.

First edition, 1987

ISBN 0-87011-857-9 (U.S.)
ISBN 4-7700-1357-4 (Japan)

# CONTENTS

2

Sishin-den, Kyoto Imperial Palace.

*Though in Kyoto*
*I long for Kyoto...*

— Basho

KYOTO: Seven Paths to the Heart of the City
by Diane Durston

# PREFACE

*To search the old is to find the new.*
                                    — Confucius


The dawn never "breaks" in Kyoto — it wouldn't dare. It proceeds cautiously down the eastern mountains with all due respect, taking great pains not to awaken the spoiled 1,200-year-old princess too roughly from her courtly dreams. The sun forgets — at moments like this — that all the princesses have gone.

Dawn in Kyoto is a time of great beauty. The restless old women rise first, rustling about with their potted plants and laundry poles, dousing the pavement at their doorsteps with water from tin ladles, making fresh the stage for this new day's busyness.

A cavernous bronze temple bell echoes through the valley in tones so somber only old men with no further use for alarm clocks awaken to its distant toll. Portly ex-soldiers stretch noisily before their bonsai shelves, shuffle gruffly off down the alley with offerings for the neighborhood shrine (the two resounding claps required to rouse the slumbering deities disturb night-owl students and sleepless writers in the process). Still in his long cotton pajamas, the balding old gentleman considers this old street nothing but a broader definition of "home." At 7 a.m., there's still an hour or so of calm left till the 20th century sets in again.

The best time to see Kyoto is at dawn — before anyone else does. Wander the old neighborhoods while the ambiguous light still blurs the concrete edges, softens the amplified voices, slows the pulse of the modern city. Only then can you understand why the Sun himself forgets there is no longer any need to tiptoe. This is the hour that brings back the legend and spirit of "the ancient capital of Japan."

# MACHINAMI — The Wooden Rowhouses of Kyoto

There are places left in Kyoto — outside the precious temple gates and touted villa walls — where the way of life of the everyday citizens goes on as if the modern circus had yet to come to town. And as with most historic cities, blind alleys and old women tell all the best stories.

Down every backstreet in Kyoto there are remnants of a way of life that is rapidly disappearing — vignettes from out of the past cling to niches and alleyways here and there throughout the city. But the economic and social changes that have taken place since the end of WWII have left their mark on the classic old neighborhoods of wooden rowhouses, the *machinami* of Kyoto. Today there are few of these neighborhoods that remain intact. Throughout most of the city traditional houses are now wedged like aching teeth between their shiny new white stucco neighbors.

This book leads you through seven historic districts — past the traditional homes, the old shops and inns, the tiny neighborhood shrines that line these narrow old streets in the heart of Kyoto. Four of these seven areas are now preserved by law; the other three have yet to be saved from the bulldozers that will almost inevitably take them, unless...

## The History of the Machinami of Kyoto

To learn something of the history of the machinami is to discover much about the history of Kyoto itself and — because Kyoto was the capital of Japan for over ten centuries — of the development of Japan as a whole historically, culturally and economically. The merchant class that arose in Kyoto during the middle ages is the basis for the economic success the country now enjoys.

The term machinami, literally "city rows," describes the physical aspect of these neighborhoods. Socially, the *o-chonai*, "the honorable inner town," is the primary unit around which these neighborhoods are organized. The *chonai-kai* is the name of the neighborhood council to which the head of every household belongs. Each *chō* consists of approximately forty homes that line the streets within about one city block.

An even smaller social increment exists within the chō, and that is the five-family unit that has been known for centuries as the *gonin-gumi*. Each family in this grouping was directly responsible for their actions to the two families on either side (whose walls often adjoined their own) as well as to the two families whose homes faced them across the narrow street. The gonin-gumi system is accredited with much

of the responsibility for the safety of Kyoto's city streets. A crime committed by a member of one family reflected on the other four in the group. In earlier days, punishment was meted out not only to individuals, but to the whole gumi. In effect, neighborhoods policed themselves, holding each other answerable for their actions.

The smallest unit was, of course, the traditional family dwelling, the *machiya*, or city house of Kyoto. Because of their long, narrow shape, the local people jokingly refer to them as *unagi no nedoko* — the bedrooms of eels. Often no more than 8 meters wide, but over 40 meters deep, this nickname is well deserved. During the Edo Period (1603-1868), taxes were levied according to the amount of frontage each building took up on the street. The owners added on to their homes from behind, until the community space that once existed in the center of every city block no longer exists today.

Every machiya is essentially constructed from a single architectural standard of measure, the size of a single *tatami* mat—about 1x2 meters. Rooms are measured by the number of mats they contain, which determines the width and length of every house. This uniform system of measurement at one time allowed for interchangeable mats and sliding doors in any house within the city of Kyoto, though now the size of tatami varies. This system also meant that not only individual houses, but the proportions of an entire neighborhood and ultimately the city as a whole could be traced back to this one small unit, making the machiya unique in the world of architecture.

## Machiya

The façade of a typical machiya in Kyoto, although styles differ from neighborhood to neighborhood, has certain interesting design features. Many houses have a curved bamboo hood that leans over the gutter in front, called an *inuyarai*, which literally means a dog barrier, though it was used as a sort of buffer to keep all kinds of pests (even the two-legged kind) and street traffic at a distance since machiya were built right on the edge of the street. Some of the houses still have a *komayose*, the now-decorative wooden railing used originally as a hitching post in the days when horses were the only means of transportation in Kyoto.

The heavy, somber façade of a typical kimono merchant's house often seems aloof at first as you approach from the street. The dark slatted windows called *kōshi*

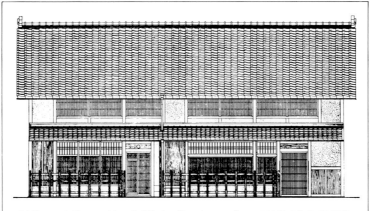

**I-1** Homes in the *machinami* of Kyoto often share walls — occasionally even roofs — with their neighbors.

*mado* are a means of creating privacy amid the bustle of city life that goes on outside just inches away. In some kinds of machiya, removable front storm doors could be opened up to reveal the room nearest the street called the *misenoma*, the shop room. Having the shop right on the street and the living quarters tucked behind afforded the owners the convenience of being able to work at home, but it naturally resulted in a lack of privacy.

Customers entered the sliding door in front and stepped into the *tōriniwa*, a stone walkway that leads back through the kitchen to the interior of the house. When the *noren* curtain was hung in place over the entry, it showed that the shop was open for business. Another curtain, often a *nawanoren*, or rope curtain, separates the kitchen from the shop front. Stepping up from the tōriniwa to the raised tatami shop room, customers sat down to discuss business over a cup of green tea with the proprietor.

Except for the tōriniwa, which often had a dirt or stone floor, all the rooms of the house were raised about two feet above ground level to provide adequate ventilation during Kyoto's humid summers. Every machiya in Kyoto is designed for the purpose of keeping cool in the summer. Though winters are cold, it is easier to bundle up than to endure the heat and humidity which sometimes lasts for four or five months. The use of woven tatami mats as flooring material throughout is said to allow the floor to "breathe." The sliding paper doors (*fusuma*) which act as room dividers are replaced with reed screens during the summer for ventilation, or can be removed completely to create as much of a breeze as possible. The rooms of machiya are lined up in a row, one behind the other, parallel to the tōriniwa, creating the "eel" effect. The division of the city into a tidy grid pattern by the Emperor Kanmu over a thousand years ago determined the long, narrow subdivision of lots within each city block.

Unlike the more spacious homes of the privileged samurai where a garden separated the entrance from the street, machiya gardens were a private, limited space located deep in the interior — always a refreshing surprise. Here the master of the house could create a small paradise of his own.

**I-2** The floor plan of this *machiya* shows the affluence of its kimono marchant owner. It is twice as wide as the average house and has two gardens where most have only one.

The homes of prosperous merchants often had more than one interior garden, one of which acted as a divider between the misenoma and the living quarters at the back. Polished wood verandas ran along the edges of these interior gardens, linking inside and out. The deep eaves made this a fine location for contemplating the harvest moon in comfort, protected from an unexpected evening shower.

The *zashiki* is the heart of the house. It is used for entertaining guests, though the function of rooms in a machiya can be changed in a moment by removing the fusuma doors that function as walls. This makes for a flexible environment, a necessity in houses in which there were often only two rooms for the many different family uses.

The zashiki is the most elegantly designed room in the house. Facing the main garden, the *okuniwa*, this room more than any other shows the influence of the tea ceremony on the machiya. Like the traditional tea room, the zashiki has a *tokonoma*, the recessed niche of honor where a single scroll painting and a flower arrangement are the only embellishments. They sit quietly in the shadows of which novelist Jun'ichiro Tanizaki once wrote so fondly: "The quality we call beauty must always grow from the realities of life, and our ancestors, forced to live in dark rooms, presently came to discover the beauty in shadows, ultimately to guide shadows to beauty's end. And so it has come to be that the beauty of a Japanese room depends on a variation of shadows, heavy shadows against light shadows...it has nothing else."

Apart from the zashiki, the most impressive room is surprisingly the kitchen. The ceiling of this room stretches high above, leaving the massive curved beams that support the heavy tile roof exposed to view. Light streams down through the skylights overhead. An old well no longer in use, sits in one corner and a large clay oven, the *kamado*, with its giant clay caldrons, squats in another. Near the oven is one of the very special features of the machiya, one to do with "soul." No machiya kitchen would be without a tiny shrine to the god of fire. The roots of ancient Japanese culture were founded in a deeply spiritual, highly super

3         *Inuyarai*      4         *Komayose*

5         *Kōshi*

6         *Kamado*

stitious tradition of paying respect to the *kami*, or gods, who protect everything from ovens to rice fields. Not to be meddled with, the kami are sure to receive their daily due of flowers and votive candles, just in case.

Dry goods and housewares were kept in long wooden cabinets called *mizuya* that lined one wall of every kitchen. Pickling, salt preservation and drying were the only means available to housewives until the refrigerator came to Kyoto in the mid 1960s.

Behind the main garden at the back of the property in the homes of most merchants was the *kura* or storehouse. The thick walls and heavy doors provided a place to keep the family treasures safe from fire and theft. Many merchants used their kura as warehouses to store goods for sale, since the small shop room in front usually provided only enough space to display samples and conduct business.

Before the ground is broken for the construction of a new house in the neighborhood, a priest from the shrine must conduct a ceremony on the site to appease the spirit of the land which just might resent another intrusion. These ceremonies are observed today, in the building of a five-story bank or a small private residence.

Geomancy, which played a principal role in former days in determining things such as the proper orientation of entrances, ovens and even toilets, is still in use today in Kyoto, though not as widely practiced as in the past. Many people still consult priests or seers for advice on the most auspicious location and orientation for their new homes.

Historically, the mini-townships (*chō*) which these homes made up united in self-defense against the constantly warring political factions that periodically left the city in ruins during the middle ages. Remnants of moats that were built originally by residents in defense of their chō can still be found in some of the old neighborhoods.

The architectural style of a particular chō was determined by the requirements of the group's trade and its proximity to a shrine or temple. The sense of community within a township was demonstrated in the unified style of elements like the type of rooftiles, the depth of the eaves, and in the pattern and number of slats in the window grates. (Styles particular to different neighborhoods will be shown in later sections dealing with each of the seven districts in this book.)

It was a breach of propriety to flaunt your personal wealth by outdoing your neighbors in the adornment of a façade, so the prosperous merchant displayed his success with lavish touches to the interior: hand-carved transoms, lacquered trims, the use of elaborately decorated paper on sliding fusuma doors, etc.

But tact and good taste were not the only considerations determining the restrained exteriors of the homes of Kyoto merchants. Strictly enforced edicts were handed down by the Shogunate during the Edo Period (1603-1868) forbidding extravagant displays in the merchants' houses, inside or outside, in an attempt to keep the rising merchant class in their place at the bottom of the social ranks. One example of the stringent laws of this period is that no merchant was allowed to build a house over two stories high. By the middle of the Edo Period, however, the merchants had achieved a powerful enough position financially to manifest their individual tastes, particularly in elements of interior design, regardless of the Shogunate and its edicts.

Another formidable enemy of the citizenry of Kyoto was fire. The long history of Kyoto reads like a list of regularly scheduled conflagrations. The Great Tenmei Fire in 1864 destroyed nearly 80% of the city. For this reason, virtually no residential structure remains in central Kyoto that is more than 120 years old.

One positive aspect of this repeated destruction and rebuilding is that the people banded together. The communities they formed each had their own special customs, rules, and architectural features that symbolized the unity of the townspeople within them.

The intrusion of modern apartment buildings, supermarkets, and parking lots into these old machinami neighborhoods has resulted in a loss of this sense of harmony, both visually and socially — a loss mourned by preservationists worldwide.

## The Historic Preservation Movement in Kyoto

Efforts at historic preservation have been undertaken by the Japanese government, but most of the legislation that exists is directed at monumental structures — at the castles, temples, shrines and villas that still grace the landscape. And, as with most historic cities of the world, Kyoto has its hands full with the restoration and maintenance of the 2,000-odd temples, shrines and villas for which this city is now world famous.

Because Kyoto was spared the bombings of World War II, the preservation of the traditional cityscape here has taken on special historical significance. The wooden dwellings that remain in Kyoto are nearly all that is left of prewar urban Japan.

Conservationist stirrings were first felt in Japan as early as the Meiji Period (1868-1912). The first conservation laws in Kyoto were passed in an effort to preserve the scenic areas on the outskirts of the city in the foothills of the mountains that surround it on three sides. Since the passing of the first law over fifty years ago, building has been prohibited on the hillsides, preserving for Kyoto the beautiful forested backdrop that these hills still provide.

In 1966, the national government passed a law aimed at the preservation of historic areas in and around former capital cities. To date, approximately 60 square kilometers of historically important landscape have been set aside (15 of which have comparatively strict development and preservation regulations). An additional 12,950 hectares of land were designated as zones of scenic beauty.

For years, emphasis was on the historic and scenic areas in the foothills surrounding the city of Kyoto. The movement to preserve historically and culturally important areas in the heart of the city came from the citizens themselves, resulting in the enactment of the Kyoto Urban Landscape Ordinance of 1972. This provided for the protection of special areas within the city by establishing guidelines for the height and design of buildings in the downtown area. Unfortunately, these guidelines are vaguely stated and have proven rather tooth-less, as evidence the eclectic cityspace with which we are faced today.

In the mid-70s citizens' groups directed their attention specifically at the machinami, the rows of traditional houses that comprise much of the densely populated central districts of Kyoto. In 1976, the first such machinami neighborhood was officially designated on a national level as a Traditional Building Preservation District — the Sanneizaka district at the foot of Kiyomizu Temple in eastern Kyoto. This was followed by Gion Shinbashi (one of the most famous of Kyoto's old geisha quarters just east of the Kamogawa River), Sagano Toriimoto (a rural village at the foot of Atago Shrine in western Kyoto), and Kamigamo Shaké-machi (an area of homes belonging to the descendants of priests of Kamigamo Shrine).

From the start, the urban preservation movement in Kyoto has placed emphasis on the preservation of entire quarters of the city. The machinami concept is essential to preservation efforts in Kyoto because the basic structure of the city — both socially and architecturally — is one of interwoven, inter-dependent parts. A 1980 census counted nearly 11,000 people per square kilometer in central Kyoto. Densely populated for centuries, a complicated and close-knit social fabric de-veloped in which every individual in a neighborhood is responsible to the others for his actions. The streets are narrow, many barely wide enough for a single car to pass, resulting in a closeness that would no doubt be disastrous in societies where individuality is the first priority. The machinami districts of Kyoto are symbols of a way of life that has evolved over the centuries in which people have learned to survive in such tight quarters — harmoniously — for so long.

The difficulty, however, of preserving whole neighbor-hoods has presented the city of Kyoto with a monumental task. Obtaining the cooperation of an entire community is the first challenge, a prospect considerably more difficult than approaching a single household. Moreover, finding a neigh-borhood that has remained relatively intact is a near impossibility for any 20th-century city, perhaps especially in Japan, where the main thrust of the whole society has been toward total modernization since the end of the last world war.

Other than the four machinami neighborhoods that have already been designated as historic preservation districts in Kyoto, it appears unlikely that other areas will be added in the future, for several reasons.

Zoning laws are extremely flexible in Kyoto, due to the traditional combination of shops, homes and cottage indus-tries within the same area. Much of the city falls under a "mixed" system of overlapping zones that has resulted in large areas classed as commercial-residential-industrial zones. As long as industry and commerce meant cottage industries like weaving and pottery, this system worked. But the economic changes that have taken place since the end of WWII brought with them problems of noise and air pollution — and the need to expand. With the high price of land in Kyoto (as much as 5 times that of a similar-sized plot in Manhattan), it is not surprising that many businesses choose to tear down their old wooden structures and rebuild 3- or 4-story concrete structures on the same long, narrow lots — resulting in the pollution and visual chaos that is evident today. The city government is now trying to encourage businesses to relocate in the less expensive southern part of the city, a move than has long been urged by preservationists.

The approach to the preservation of the machinami dis-tricts in Kyoto has been to provide guidelines for renovations to ensure that they continue to thrive as living, working neighborhoods, rather than as museum pieces. With the help of architects at Kyoto University, residents have also been given access to historically accurate models for restorations within the four specially designated areas mentioned above. Exterior changes to buildings must conform to the archi-tectural style of the area, but, in order to accommodate the changing patterns of contemporary life, the owner is free to re-model the interior to suit his needs.

A few individual dwellings have become recognized a "Bunkazai," or Cultural Assets, a category that qualifies them for preservation assistance on a national level. In such cases, both interior and exterior must be preserved intact or meticulously restored to original condition. The lack of modern conveniences (inadequate heating, cooking and toilet facilities) in the traditional machiya makes life ex-tremely difficult in the 20th century. Owners of these homes receive a part of the cost of renovation from the government, as do residents of preserved districts, but no tax allowance are made in either case. Many owners therefore decline government offers to have their homes honored with this title.

The current climate among much of the population of Kyoto for further modernization and for more individuality and freedom of expression is understandable, given the poverty and repression of the past. While half the population is enthusiastic about saving the traditional character of Kyoto, the other half sees the old wooden dwellings as dinosaurs — anomalies that have outlived their time. In fact, so much has already been destroyed that the traditional image of Kyoto that tourists, both at home and abroad, have been led to expect is rapidly becoming more legend than reality.

If preservationists were motivated simply by a nostalgic desire to cling to a past that seems more romantic in retrospect than it ever really was, developers could easily dismiss their attempts as sentimental and old-fashioned. More important (to use the cliché of a very distant cousin) is the importance of ensuring that "the baby doesn't get tossed out with the bathwater" — that the way of life to which these old neighborhoods gave shelter — the cooperation, the safety, and the sense of pride does not disappear with each old wooden home that ends in a pile of dust.

# SEVEN PATHS
# TO THE HEART OF THE CITY

Sunlight breaks through the clowds over Kyoto.

# SANNEIZAKA

## ［産寧坂］

8

*All of us are pilgrims on this earth.*
*I've even heard it said that the earth itself is a pilgrim in the heavens.*

— Maxim Gorky, 1903

*Pilgrim* — a person who travels a long distance to some sacred place; a traveler or wanderer. For over twelve centuries pilgrims have made their way up the sloping cobblestone paths at the foot of the mountains in the east of Kyoto to Kiyomizu-dera. Founded in the eighth century, before Kyoto became the capital of Japan, this temple is for everyone. For women who pray for an easy childbirth, for ascetics who stand in midwinter under the icy waters of Otowa-no-taki, for devotees of the eleven-headed goddess, Kannon...for young women who come to buy charms for luck in matters of love at Jishu Gongen, the shrine that adjoins Kiyomizu. For travelers, worshippers and school girls — this is Mecca for pilgrims in Japan.

The Sanneizaka district, named after one of the old cobbled streets that leads up the hill to Kiyomizu-dera, is a *monzenchō* — a town that grew up outside the gates of a temple. Centuries ago, the shops along these slopes catered to the needs of pilgrims, providing a cup of tea, a string of prayer beads, a memento of the journey, and perhaps a bit of local advice on seeing the sights...much as they do today. In 1976, Sanneizaka became the first urban neighborhood in Japan to be officially designated as a historic preservation district.

Start at Yasaka Jinja and follow the path that leads to Ishibe-kōji, a backstreet so narrow that in places they say you can touch both sides at once. The high stone walls that line this cobbled path lead through a short maze of former villas, turned teahouses and inns. Here the geisha of Gion entertain their guests each evening behind reed screen curtains in this exclusive, reclusive neighborhood — a quiet time-warp to slip into on your way to Ninenzaka.

Ninenzaka is the name of the stone-paved path that leads to Sanneizaka, often called "Sannenzaka" to match it. Ninenzaka means two-year slope, and Sannenzaka means three-year slope. Local superstition has it that a slip on the steps between them means two or three years of bad luck. Purchasing a good luck gourd (if it isn't already too late) at the gourd shop beside the steps is said to help. Watch your step, as the saying goes.

The shops and homes in this area are among the oldest *machiya*, or city dwellings, in Kyoto, since the area east of the Kamogawa River was spared much of the damage suffered by the rest of the capital from the frequent fires that plagued the city. *Mushiko-mado* windows are characteristic of one of the oldest styles of architecture that still exists in Kyoto. These slatted second-floor windows seem to be cut out of the clay walls themselves, and legend has it that in feudal times, when commoners were forced to prostrate themselves before passing warlords, these windows permitted ambitious merchants to keep "a head above" their landlords, observing them secretly from their hidden vantage point as they passed through the streets below. Other less romantic observers suggest that ventilation was the primary concern...but a stroll up Sanneizaka is no time for deductive reasoning.

During the sixteenth century, a number of potters opened

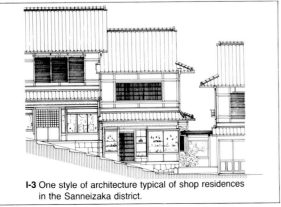

I-3 One style of architecture typical of shop residences in the Sanneizaka district.

shop in the Sanneizaka district, and the fine hand-painte porcelain ware for which they became famous is calle Kiyomizu-yaki. Because Kyoto was for ten centuries th home of the Imperial Court, the local pottery has a high decorative flair that reflects the tastes of the old aristocrac Although the kilns have been moved to Yamashina, to th east of Kyoto, many still keep studios and shops here at th foot of Kiyomizu-dera. Visit the home of Kawai Kanjiro, th noted potter-philosopher and cofounder of the Ming (Folk Art) Movement that sparked enough interest in han made folk items to save many struggling craft villages Japan in the 1930s. His home (see map) is open to the publi Although the exterior was designed to match the neig

...orhood style, Kawai designed the interior in the style of ...farmhouse of the Hida-Takayama district in Nagano ...refecture. This quiet potter's studio and kiln are full of the ...pirit of this remarkable man.

The spire of the three-storied pagoda at Kiyomizu-dera pierces the sky — a cosmic antenna to the Dainichi Nyorai, the Buddha of the beginningless and endless ultimate reality.

The main hall of Kiyomizu-dera houses an eleven-faced, thousand-armed image of Kannon, the Buddhist deity of mercy, that is shown only once every thirty-three years. The 33 different forms Kannon can take to save mankind have led pilgrims up the slopes of Sanneizaka to Kiyomizu-dera — the 16th in the famous Pilgrimage of Thirty-Three Kannon Temples — for over eleven centuries.

**10** Shops along Sanneizaka. The *mushiko-mado* (or insect-cage windows) on the second floor allowed shopkeepers to observe passing warlords from above, a pleasure otherwise forbidden to members of their class in the feudal ages.

**11** Kiyomizu-yaki, ceramics from the Kiyomizu district, reflect the tastes of the imperial court, whose presence influenced the arts and crafts of Kyoto for over ten centuries.

**11**

清水 二年坂

I-4 An 18th-century woodblock print of the *monzench* or temple gate town, whose tea shops have serve pilgrims on their way to Kiyomizu-dera for mar centuries. The *nobori-gama*, or climbing kilns, in the foreground once produced the *Kiyomizu-yaki* cer mics for which this district is famous.

12

**12** A tea shop beside the steps of Ninenzaka.

**13** The home of potter Kawai Kanjirō, a founder of the Folk Art Movement in the 1930s. A visit to his quiet home, workshop and kiln restores faith in the importance of things made by hand.

**14** Ishibe-kōji, a quiet backstreet lined with tradit inns and teahouses — a little-known part of the tertainment world of nearby Gion.

13

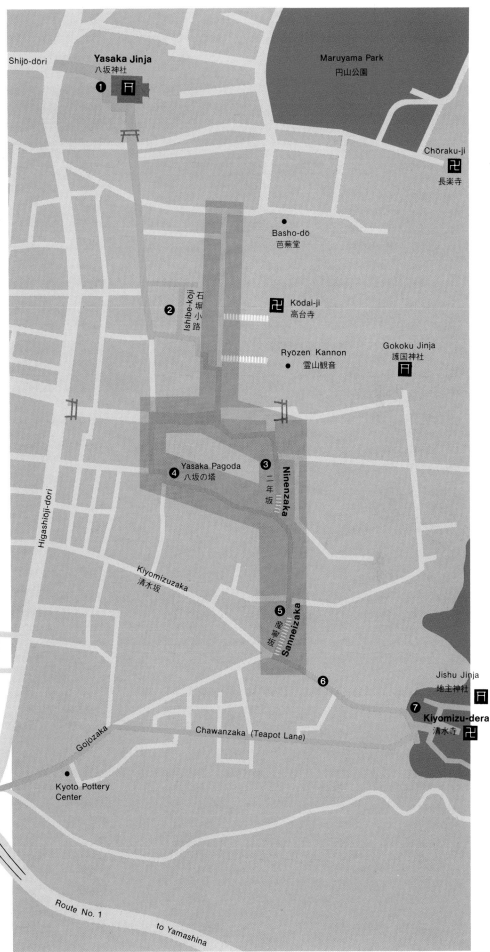

**ANNEIZAKA** （産寧坂）

**ETTING THERE:** Take City Bus No. 11 or 12 from
njō Keihan Station. Get off at "Yasaka Jinja mae".
twenty-minute walk from Sanjō Keihan Station, or
minutes by taxi.

**UGGESTED COURSE:** ❶ Yasaka Jinja → ❷ Ishibe-
i → ❸ Ninenzaka → ❹ Yasaka Pagoda →
Sanneizaka → ❻ Kiyomizuzaka → ❼ Kiyomizu-dera
❽ Kawai Kanjirō Memorial House (time permitting)

**OR THE TAXI DRIVER:**
八坂神社前まで行ってください。"
asaka Jinja mae madé itte-kudasai.)
ease take me to the front of Yasaka Shrine.
bout ¥500 from Sanjō keihan Station.)

**STIMATED TIME:** Half a day.

: The preserved districts are
indicated in gray.

Shijō-dori

**Yasaka Jinja**
八坂神社
❶ 冊

Maruyama Park
円山公園

Chōraku-ji
卍
長楽寺

Basho-dō
芭蕉堂

❷ 石塀小路 Ishibe-kōji

Kōdai-ji
卍
高台寺

Ryōzen Kannon
霊山観音

Gokoku Jinja
護国神社
冊

❹ Yasaka Pagoda
八坂の塔

❸ Ninenzaka
二年坂

Higashiōji-dori

Kiyomizuzaka
清水坂

❺ Sanneizaka
産寧坂

Jishu Jinja
地主神社
冊

❻

❼ **Kiyomizu-dera**
清水寺
卍

Gojōzaka

Chawanzaka (Teapot Lane)

Kyoto Pottery
Center

Gojō-dori

❽
Kawai Kanjirō
Memorial House

Route No. 1

to Yamashina

# GION SHINBASHI
## ［祇園・新橋］

**15**

Gion was made for watery dreams. Behind its latticed doorways and windows lives a world that few are privileged to know...a world for men, wealthy men...run by women, the geisha of Gion. Yoshii Isamu's poem (see page 16), carved in stone beside the Shirakawa Canal that flows through this district, almost became its epitaph. But the women of Gion would never permit that. In its heyday there were hundreds of geisha in the district. Today only about fifty remain, but as professional entertainers they are among the strongest advocates of maintaining the customs and traditions of Kyoto. Kyoto dialect, lilting and evasive, is spoken in Gion...almost religiously...and almost nowhere else as pervasively. Shamisen lessons are attended every morning, and traditional dance is kept alive and vital here.

The men who visit Gion are still catered to — shamelessly pampered, in fact — here behind the *sudare* reed screens that hide this private world of luxury from public view. The privileged few play out their private fantasies here in an elegant atmosphere in which the nuance of meaning in a glance, like the nape of neck, is more seductive in the Japanese erotic sensibility than any outright declaration of love...or lust.

Gion is still very much a mystery. It is the home of the "water trade," the "floating world" of ukiyo-e prints, in which languid, sad-eyed women draped in hand-painted kimono mourned the coming of dawn — and the inevitable loss of love this evanescent life of passion promised them. What goes on behind the *bengara-gōshi*, as the rust-colored latticed windows of Gion are known? No one can (or will) say for sure...mystery, after-all, is the key to its seductive charm.

Shinbashi is actually the name of a small bridge built in the early eighteenth century over the Shirakawa River in the northern part of Gion, but the triangular block of *o-chaya* or teahouses, beside it shares its name. O-chaya, are the places to which geisha (or *geiko*, as they are known in Kyoto) are called to entertain guests. No stranger gains admittance to an o-chaya in Gion; no amount of money takes the place of a formal introduction by a trusted regular guest.

*Maiko* are the apprentice geisha, the painted dolls you might see clip-clopping on high platform *pokkori geta* with their elaborate brocade sashes trailing behind them, if you stroll through Shinbashi just after sunset. Eighteen, nineteen, twenty years old, the maiko-san are the icing on the evening cake in Gion. While the geiko she accompanies carries the conversation (notoriously sprinkled with wit and double entendre) the maiko poses and plays her pouty parlor game, pouring the saké and pealing the grapes for "*danna*," the "lord and master," the honored guest who might one day become her own special benefactor.

Yet the geisha of Gion are not prostitutes. The mere mention of such a notion is guaranteed to arouse an indignant response in this neighborhood. They are performers, entertainers, as the character *gei* (芸) implies. As such, they are responsible to this day for keeping many of the traditional performing arts alive in modern Japan. That is one reason why Gion Shinbashi is unique as a historic preservation area. Here, the history that is being preserved is still a vital part of the present. The mystique of the floating world lives on in Gion.

Ichiriki, the three-hundred-year-old o-chaya that stands on the corner of Shijō and Hanami-kōji, has become a legendary symbol of Gion. It was here that Oishi Yoshio (1659-1703) the leader of the 47 Rōnin, pretended to lose himself in a life

17

of debauchery while secretly plotting his revenge against the lord responsible for his master's death. The dusky red color of the walls of Ichiriki, once characteristic of the whole Gion district, are now scarcely found anywhere else.

The Minamiza Kabuki Theater, beside the Kamogawa River on Shijō-dōri, dates to the early 17th century and is the oldest theater in Japan. The present building was constructed in 1929, but is full of the original spirit of Kabuki, with galleries full of passionate devotees in December when the Kaomise (Face Showing) Festival is held each year. Major stars from all over Japan "put in an appearance" on stage the Minamiza during this month-long event. Kabuki began in Kyoto in the seventeenth century, when a young woman known as Izumo-no-Okuni danced on the banks of the river here before a crowd of enthusiastic fans.

18

*Kani kaku ni*
*Gion wa koishi.*
*Neru toki mo*
*makura no shita ni*
*mizu no nagaruru.*

*No matter what they say,*
*I love Gion.*
*Even in my sleep,*
*the sound of water*
*flows beneath my pillow.*

— Yoshii Isamu (1886-1960)

15 The nape of a neck — a subtle gesture of traditional Japanese eroticism, an art perfected by the *maiko* of Gion.

16 Nightfall at the *o-chaya*, the "teahouses" where geisha (or *geiko*, as they are known in Kyoto) entertain their guests.

17 Reed screens conceal from public view the "floating world" of teahouses along the Shirakawa Canal Gion.

19 A narrow *rōji*, or passageway, between rows of teahouses along backstreets in the heart of Gion.

16

20

20 A pair of *maiko*, or apprentice geisha, on their way to entertain guests at a teahouse in Gion.

21 An ornate *obidome* clasp, one of the only kinds of jewelry traditionally worn by Japanese women, decorates a maiko's *obi* sash.

21

22

I-5 The architectural style typical of teahouses in the Gion Shinbashi district.

3

2 Outside Ichiriki, one of the most famous teahouses in Japan. The rust-colored walls are characteristic of this entertainment district. Note the bamboo-slatted *inuyarai*, or "dog barrier," a device to protect the façades of Kyoto-style houses built right on the edge of the street.

3 The light of day turns Gion Shinbashi into a quiet, traditional neighborhood, the trappings of the 20th century lost in the snow.

## GION SHINBASHI （祇園・新橋）

**GETTING THERE:** Gion Shinbashi is a short walk from the downtown area. From Sanjō Keihan station, walk south on Nawate-dōri past the many antique shops and restaurants there, until you come to the Shira-kawa Canal. Turn left and you are in the Shinbashi district.

**SUGGESTED COURSE:** ❶ Nawate-dōri → ❷ Shira-kawa Canal → ❸ "Kani kaku ni" stone → ❹ Shinbashi Bridge → ❺ O-chaya, or teahouses → ❻ Ichiriki O-chaya → ❼ Gion Corner (evening shows featuring demon-strations of Japanese arts) → ❽ Minamiza Theater

**FOR THE TAXI DRIVER:**
"縄手通りの白川橋まで行ってください。"
(Nawate-dōri no Shirakawa-bashi madé itte-kudasai.)
Please take me to the Shirakawa Bridge on Nawate Street.

**ESTIMATED TIME:** One hour (not including the hour it takes to see the show at Gion Corner).

▨ : The preserved districts are indicated in gray.

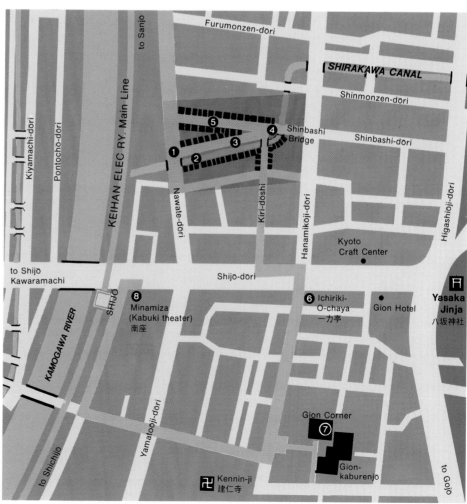

# SAGANO TORIIMOTO
## ［嵯峨野・鳥居本］

24

*In the suburbs of Kyoto, a form of roof and ridge...may often be seen.*
*In this form the supplementary roof is more sharply defined; the corners of it are slightly*
*turned up as in the temple roof. To be more definite, the main roof, which is a*
*hipped roof, has built upon it a low upper-roof, which is a gable;*
*and upon this rests, like a separate structure, a continuous saddle of thatch,*
*having upon its back a few bamboos running longitudinally,*
*and across the whole a number of narrow saddles of thatch sheathed with bark,*
*and over all a long bamboo bound to the ridge with cords.*
*These roofs, broad and thick eaved, with their deep-set, heavily latticed smoke windows,*
*and the warm brown thatch, form a pleasing contrast to the thin-shingled*
*roofs of the poorer neighboring houses.*

— Edward S. Morse, 1887

The "poorer neighboring houses" Morse referred to a hundred years ago no longer exist in Sagano. But fortunately a few of the magnificent thatched country homes he so admired do remain and are preserved in this area by law. Around the turn of the century, most of the houses in the countryside in Japan were thatched. Today there are not very many left—they are considered fire hazards, for one thing— for another, they are too difficult to repair. The special type of reed used is becoming harder and harder to obtain, and the days when an entire community gathered to help rebuild one farmer's rooftop are all but forgotten. The handful of thatched roofs that remain on the old road leading up to the bright vermilion gateway (*torii*) of Atago Jinja are a symbol of rural Kyoto — the way it was.

Atago Jinja is a steep two-hour hike straight up the side of Mt. Atago in the western part of Kyoto. The God Who Prevents Fires lives there, and for several centuries, the citizens of Kyoto have trudged dutifully up the steps to kee their city safe from the flames that destroyed it time and agai in the past.

At one time the entire city of Kyoto was built of nothin but wood, thatch and tiles, and people lived with th constant threat of fire. The red plastic fire buckets you se outside the doors of many old houses in Kyoto today are reminder of the danger of fire. Because the rowhouses c Kyoto share wooden walls with their neighbors on both side: my fire is your fire. So once a month, everyone marched u Mt. Atago to pray.

It was a long, arduous climb. But at the foot of th mountain, at either side of the torii, stand the two thatche teahouses, Tsuta-ya and Hirano-ya, that have offered refresh ment to weary climbers for 400 years. *Shinko dango* is th name of the kind of sweet rice cakes served with tea here. I more recent years, both teahouses have become famous fo

26

28

their *ayu* cuisine, a small freshwater fish served as the main course of this traditional Kyoto-style meal. Ayu are caught fresh each morning and charcoal grilled in traditional country style. The aroma of smoked fish, the view of the maple trees over the pond, the atmosphere of an authentic country farmhouse...all well worth the walk.

The road down from Toriimoto leads past Adashino Nenbutsu-ji, with the hundreds of stone Buddhas that mark the graves of nameless men and women who died penniless...or simply forgotten...centuries ago — Kyoto's boot hill. There are many tiny temples along the way, like Giō-ji, where a famed beauty, the banished mistress of a Shogun, lived out her life in the nunnery. A poet's hut, Rakushi-sha, where Basho himself spent time with a friend during his travels...all the way to Arashiyama beside the Oi gawa River, where the Togetsu-kyō Bridge marks the former playground of emperors and warlords. Far from the palace in Kyoto, the Sagano district of Kyoto has always been famous for its lush bamboo forests, steep-walled ravines, quiet rice fields, and legends of romance.

6 Architectural drawing of rural houses in the Sagano Toriimoto district.

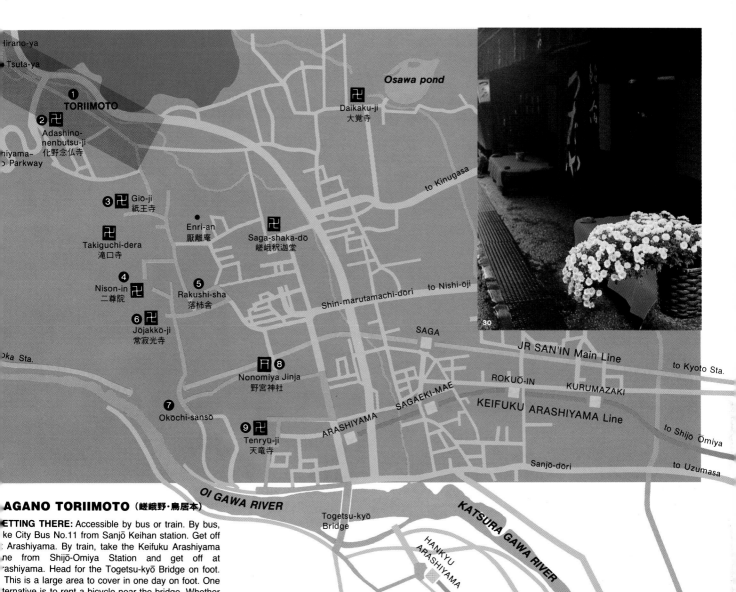

Hirano-ya

Tsuta-ya

**①**
**TORIIMOTO**

**②** 卍
Adashino-
nenbutsu-ji
化野念仏寺

...hiyama–
...o Parkway

**③** 卍 Giō-ji
祇王寺

• Enri-an
厭離庵

卍
Takiguchi-dera
滝口寺

Saga-shaka-dō
嵯峨釈迦堂 卍

Daikaku-ji
大覚寺 卍

Osawa pond

to Kinugasa

**④** Nison-in 卍
二尊院

**⑤**
Rakushi-sha
落柿舎

Shin-marutamachi-dori

to Nishi-ōji

**⑥** 卍
Jōjakkō-ji
常寂光寺

...ka Sta.

SAGA

JR SAN'IN Main Line

to Kyoto Sta.

**⑧** 卍
Nonomiya Jinja
野宮神社

ROKUŌ-IN

KURUMAZAKI

**⑦**
Okōchi-sansō

SAGAEKI-MAE

KEIFUKU ARASHIYAMA Line

to Shijō Ōmiya

**⑨** 卍
Tenryū-ji
天竜寺

ARASHIYAMA

Sanjō-dori

to Uzumasa

OI GAWA RIVER

KATSURA GAWA RIVER

Togetsu-kyō
Bridge

HANKYU
ARASHIYAMA

## ...AGANO TORIIMOTO（嵯峨野・鳥居本）

**...ETTING THERE:** Accessible by bus or train. By bus, ...ke City Bus No.11 from Sanjō Keihan station. Get off ... Arashiyama. By train, take the Keifuku Arashiyama ...ne from Shijō-Omiya Station and get off at ...rashiyama. Head for the Togetsu-kyō Bridge on foot. ...This is a large area to cover in one day on foot. One ...ternative is to rent a bicycle near the bridge. Whether ...y rented bicycle (¥800 per day) or taxi (¥500 from the ...idge to Toriimoto), it is a good idea to go straight up ...Sagano Toriimoto and work your way slowly back ...wn to Arashiyama.

**...UGGESTED COURSE:** ① Toriimoto → ② Adashino ...enbutsu-ji → ③ Giō-ji → ④ Nison-in → ⑤ Rakushi-...a → ⑥ Jōjakkō-ji → ⑦ Okōchi-sansō (the villa of ...former silent movie star) → ⑧ Nonomiya Jinja → ...Tenryū-ji → ⑩ Togetsu-kyō Bridge

**...OR THE TAXI DRIVER:**

...山の渡月橋まで行ってください。"

...rashiyama no Togetsu-kyō madé itte-kudasai.)

...ease take me to the Togetsu-kyō Bridge in ...rashiyama.

...bout ¥1,700 from the downtown area.)

**...STIMATED TIME:** One full day.

▦ : The preserved districts are indicated in gray.

Candles lit in prayer before the graves of thousands of unknown souls in the cemetery beside Adashino Nenbutsu-ji.

/27 Lush green and brilliant crimson in the forests of Sagano — the last of rural Kyoto.

The thatched roof of a teahouse in Sagano-Toriimoto, serving refreshments for over 400 years to worshippers on their way up the mountain to Ata-go Jinga.

Harvest time in the ricefields of Sagano.

Beneath the shady eaves of a teahouse in Sagano-Toriimoto.

Pleasure boat on the Oi gawa River in Arashiyama.

31

# KAMIGAMO SHAKÉ-MACHI
## ［上賀茂・社家町］

32

The goddess Tamayori-hime led an extremely exciting life. While bathing in a river one day in northern Kyoto, she noticed a bright-red arrow floating in the water toward her and couldn't resist taking it home with her. For good luck, she tucked it under her pillow that night...only to be awakened at midnight to find that the arrow had turned into a dashing young man..."and she became pregnant," as the famous legend discreetly puts it. This was to be only the first of the surprises in store for her Heavenly Highness.

She gave birth to the God of Thunder, Wakeikazuchi, who burst from her womb to explode through the rooftop into the night sky. He became the deity of thunder and rain, and dwells to this day in all his celestial impetuousness at Kamigamo Jinja.

Kamigamo Jinja was originally the personal shrine of the Kamo family, who inhabited this valley for centuries before the Emperor Kanmu built his capital here in 794. By the time Kanmu arrived, the God to Thunder had already earned himself quite a reputation for his violent temper, the apparent cause of continual floods and storms that plagued the area. The Emperor Kanmu made sure that his emissary always paid respects at Kamigamo Jinja during Aoi Matsuri, the special festival that was established in the sixth century to appease the unpredictable god. To this day, an imperial messenger proceeds from the former palace to the shrine in an elaborate procession with ox-drawn carts to pray for peace and an abundant harvest every year on the 5th of May. Until the 13th century, a virgin princess from the imperial family was always in attendance at Kamigamo, where the lusty legend of the Thunder God's birth had won him a consequent role as the God of Fertility.

Kamigamo Jinja is one of the oldest and most revered in Kyoto, and the priests whose families have attended it fo centuries dwelt in the neighborhood that surrounds it — th *shaké-machi* of Kamigamo. The stream that runs through th grounds of the shrine is sacred, and the priests built thei homes along its banks just outside the precincts of the shrine

If you follow the stream down the narrow road runnin east of Kamigamo, you pass the clay-walled shaké-mach homes, one of which, the Nishimura House, is a histori landmark which is open to the public (except in midwinter You'll find that the stream has been channeled through th classic Heian-style garden of this and all the shaké-mach homes. The resident priest bathed in a small, but deep, poo of water from this stream before proceeding to the shrine fo official ceremonies. There were once over 275 shaké-mach households in the Kamigamo district. By the 17th centur they had formed a tightly knit township around the shrine and were both under its spiritual protection and responsib for defending it in times of trouble. A system of moat encircled the town during the feudal ages to help defend from fires and wars, as well as for irrigation.

The shaké-machi homes are open and spacious compare to the city dwellings in the middle of Kyoto, where land is such a premium. Outside the original city boundaries at th foot of the Kitayama Mountains, the Kamigamo shaké machi sits amidst rice fields and vegetable gardens. *Kamo nasu*, a special round variety of eggplant that is a popula treat in Kyoto, is still grown in this area, and it is not unusu to see women from the Kamigamo district pulling heavy cart through the streets in midtown selling vegetables they hav grown themselves.

Pickles, or *tsukemono*, are another specialty of thi district, and along Kusunoki-dōri (which takes its name fro

I-7 Architectural drawing of the homes of shrine priests in the Kamigamo Shaké-machi districts.

36

the giant *kusunoki*, or camphor tree, around which it winds) you'll find Narita, one of Kyoto's finest pickle shops. Note the high ceiling with its rough-hewn post-and-beam construction held together by an elaborate joinery system without the use of nails. Make your way past the tiny neighborhood shrine, Ota Jinja, farther east — where people come to pray for good health, luck in marriage, and even success on the stage. The pond beside it is filled with iris during the month of May, attracting scores of avid photographers each year. Beyond the pond is Azekura, a 300-year-old saké warehouse that was moved to this site all the way from Nara twenty years ago. The huge structure becomes an exhibition hall occasionally for kimono shows, but is known for its fine home-style *soba* noodle soup year round.

Time and water are two of the elements that make Kamigamo special among the old neighborhoods of Kyoto. Older than the city of Kyoto itself, this neighborhood has retained much of its quiet atmosphere because it has managed to stay somehow on the fringe. The waters of Nara-no-Ogawa stream that flow through the shaké-machi here recall the traditional Japanese reverence for water as a source of purification...both of body and soul.

**32** Corridors of Kamigamo Jinja, one of Kyoto's oldest shrines.

**33** Symbols of the "twin peaks of heaven" in the sand gardens of Kamigamo Jinja.

**34** The clay walls of the Kamigamo *shaké-machi*, the homes of Shinto priest families connected with Kamigamo Jinja, along the sacred canal.

**35** Iris in full bloom in the pond at Ota Jinja.

**36** A "treasure boat from heaven" — a New Year's ornament displayed at Kamigamo Jinja as a symbol of good fortune in the coming year.

35

39

37 Soaking pickle barrels in the Kamogawa River near Kamigamo.

38 Women preparing *suguki*, a root vegetable related to the turnip, for the making of pickles in Kamigamo.

39 A farm woman pulling her heavy cart of vegetables door-to-door in the Kamigamo district.

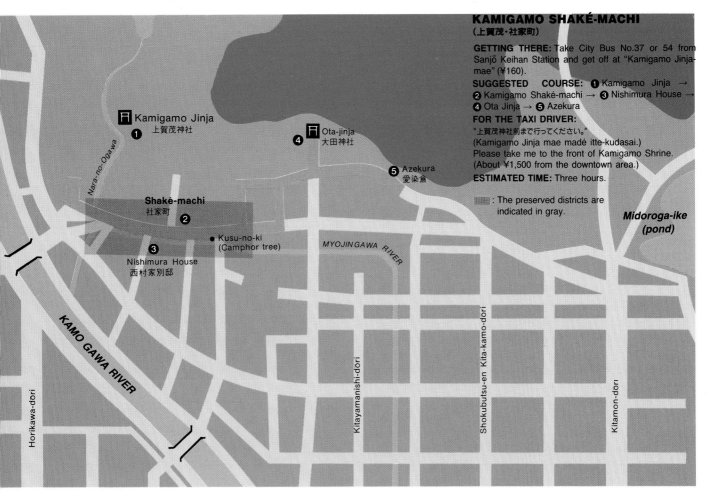

### KAMIGAMO SHAKÉ-MACHI
（上賀茂・社家町）

**GETTING THERE:** Take City Bus No.37 or 54 from Sanjō Keihan Station and get off at "Kamigamo Jinja-mae" (¥160).

**SUGGESTED COURSE:** ❶ Kamigamo Jinja → ❷ Kamigamo Shaké-machi → ❸ Nishimura House → ❹ Ota Jinja → ❺ Azekura

**FOR THE TAXI DRIVER:**
"上賀茂神社前まで行ってください。"
(Kamigamo Jinja mae madé itte-kudasai.)
Please take me to the front of Kamigamo Shrine.
(About ¥1,500 from the downtown area.)

**ESTIMATED TIME:** Three hours.

▒▒▒ : The preserved districts are indicated in gray.

*Midoroga-ike (pond)*

🅷 Kamigamo Jinja
上賀茂神社
❶

🅷 Ota-jinja
大田神社
❹

Azekura
愛染倉
❺

Nara-no-Ogawa

**Shaké-machi**
社家町
❷

● Kusu-no-ki
(Camphor tree)

*MYOJINGAWA RIVER*

❸
Nishimura House
西村家別邸

KAMO GAWA RIVER

Horikawa-dōri

Kitayamanishi-dōri

Shokubutsu-en Kita-kamo-dōri

Kitamon-dōri

# NISHIJIN
[西陣]

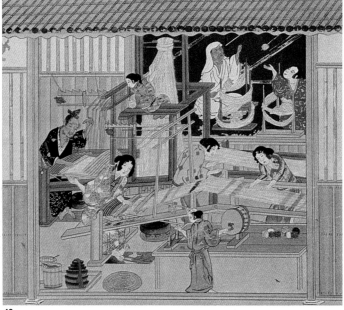

40

*Kattan, kotton...kattan, kotton...kattan, kotton...* the endless rattle of 20,000 weavers' looms beats out a pattern that is centuries old — the street music of Nishijin. The word for loom in Japanese is *hata*, perhaps because these weavers were descendants of the Hata family, Chinese immigrants who brought their craft to Kyoto before the Imperial Court moved to this valley in 794.

The Nishijin district is in the northwestern corner of Kyoto, and though the boundaries are not clearly defined, it stretches roughly east to west from Horikawa to Nishiōji, and north to south from Kitaōji to Ichijō.

Although this district has been the center of the traditional textile industry in Kyoto since the middle ages, there is no "Nishijin" on the map. The name means "Western Camp" because the empty field where the weavers' guild decided to set up their looms at the end of the devastating Onin Wars in 1477 had been the official encampment of the Western Army.

This thriving merchant's district has survived the subsequent series of natural and manmade disasters that have visited the city of Kyoto over the centuries. It is not an officially recognized preservation district...and, unless something is done soon, Nishijin will almost inevitably lose its traditional character, as has much of the rest of this city.

Behind the tightly slatted *senbon-gōshi*, or thousand-fingered latticed windows, the production of elaborate gold brocade and silk damask goes on — for the time being — as it always has, almost anonymously. Catching a glimpse of dyers hanging their colorful threads from poles between the rafters in the back rooms may be all you'll see...or following the clack and rattle of the looms to an open doorway in summer, you might get a peek down the breezeway of a Nishijin weaver working at her loom.

Though much of the fabric produced since the turn of t[h] century has been done on Western-style Jacquard loom[s] there are as many as 2,000 traditional-style looms left [in] Nishijin today. One of the most complicated and tim[e] consuming types of weaving done in Nishijin is call[ed] *tsuzure-ori*, a process in which the weaver files grooves in h[er] fingernails to separate the weave and draw the weft tig[ht] enough to achieve the intricate pictorial quality for which t[he] fabric is known.

In accordance with tradition, no one person produces a[ny] finished fabric from start to finish alone. Dozens of separa[te] craftsmen are contracted, each performing one of the ma[ny] steps of the weaving process. One family dyes the threa[d,] another threads the looms, one weaves, another stretch[es.] There are even people in Nishijin that specialize only [in] steaming newly completed fabrics — or simply in carryi[ng] works in process from one household to the next.

Finally, the *obi* sashes and kimono of Nishijin are so[ld] under the name of one of the wholesalers in the district wh[o] contract the individual craftsmen. These wholesalers are t[he] classic "middlemen" in Japanese business. Names li[ke] Daimaru, Takashimaya, and Mitsui were all origina[l] kimono merchants from Nishijin.

41
42

Kitano Jinja is located in Nishijin, about a block east of Nishi-ōji on Imadegawa. It was established in the tenth century and is dedicated to Sugawara no Michizane, a poet, scholar, and Imperial Minister. Today, Kitano is the patron saint of students who flock here each year to pray for success in their entrance exams. It is also the site of a flea market popular for its antiques, on the 25th of each month. This fair also attracts farmers from outlying districts, as well as Kyotoites, who come to Tenjin-san (as the flea market is most commonly known) to look for bargains in tools, clothing and foods as they have for centuries.

Just a block east of the shrine is a geisha quarter known a Kamishichiken, an area which is older than both Gion an Shimabara. The name refers to the first "seven houses" in th

eighborhood that were said to have been originally con-
ructed of wood left over from repairs to Kitano Jinja in
he Muromachi Period (1334-1568). The triangular block of
ahouses here is less frequented today than the entertain-
ent districts downtown, making this a quiet place to stroll.

46

5

**40** A 17th-century woodblock print depicting the weavers of Nishijin.

**41/42** Dyed silk threads and handwoven brocades — the colors and patterns of Nishijin, for over six centuries the center of fine textile production in Japan.

**43** Tiled rooftops still prevail in Nishijin — but for how much longer?

**44** Children at play in the narrow backstreets of Nishijin.

**45** The *noren* curtain announces this as an *obi* weaver's shop in Nishijin.

**46** Flowers decorate the doorways of traditional homes at New Year's in Nishijin.

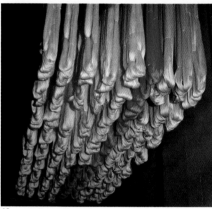

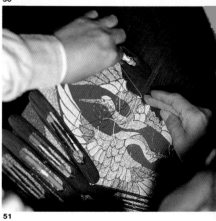

47 A gorgeous hand-woven *Nishijin-ori* brocade sash

48 An artist draws the outline to be dyed on silk.

49 Dyed silk threads hanging out to dry.

50 Weaving in progress.

51 *Tsuzure-ori*, or fingernail-weaving as it is sometimes called.

53

52

52 Children play a traditional New Year's game in Nishijin.

53 Potted gardens clinging to the edge of the street in this densely populated neighborhood.

## NISHIJIN (西 陣)

**GETTING THERE:** Take City Bus No. 8, 10 or 51 from Sanjō Keihan Station, and get off at Kitano Jinja.

**SUGGESTED COURSE:** ❶ Kitano Jinja (if you visit the flea market on the 25th of the month, get there early in the morning) → ❷ Kamishichiken teahouses → ❸ Senbon-shaka-dō → ❹ Honryū-ji → ❺ the heart of Nishijin → ❻ Nishijin Textile Center

**FOR THE TAXI DRIVER:**

"北野神社前まで行ってください。"

(Kitano Jinja mae madé itte-kudasai.)

Please take me to the front of Kitano Shrine.

(About ¥1,500 from the downtown area.)

**ESTIMATED TIME:** Half a day.

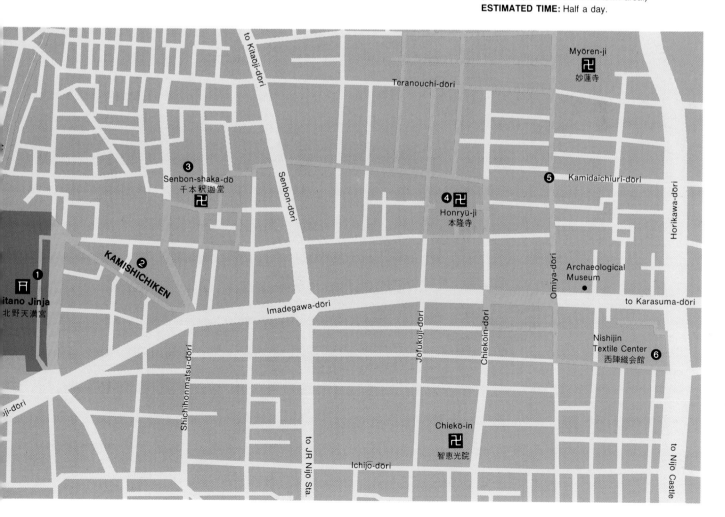

# HONGANJI/SHIMABARA
## ［本願寺・島原］

**54**

The great, curved expanse of gray tile rooftops that belong to the two temples known as Nishi-(west) and Higashi-(east) Honganji is the first glimpse of the former capital for most visitors arriving at Kyoto Station. As headquarters of two schools of the still powerful and popular Jōdo Shinshu sect of Buddhism, they are the home of Amida, the Buddha of the Western Paradise, whose devotees need only chant his name to find salvation.

Nishi-Honganji is the more interesting of the two temples. Moved here in the late 16th century by the great military leader Toyotomi Hideyoshi, the impressive structures contain a number of masterpieces of Momoyama Period (1583-1600) art. Higashi-Honganji was built in 1603 by Tokugawa Ieyasu to attract followers away from the western temple in order to divide the power (one of his favorite tactics) of the powerful sect, but the original buildings were unfortunately destroyed by fire and the present structure dates from 1895.

The neighborhood between the two temples is exemplary of a *jinaichō*, or "town inside the precincts of a temple." The road along which it stands was once a part of the grounds of Nishi-Honganji. The Honganji district has been the center for the production of religious articles — Buddhist carvings, prayer beads, bronze bells, wooden drums, incense and candles — for over four hundred years.

One of the most interesting religious objects produced in the workshops of the Honganji district are the *butsudan*, the Buddhist altars made for worship in the home. These are the wooden cabinets that hold the name tablets of ancestors, and they have a prominent place in the main room of many devout Buddhist families. The dark lacquered exterior opens up to reveal an often brilliantly gilded interior decorated with glittering golden ornaments, candleholders and lanterns in a style that makes rococo seem tame.

Each sect of Buddhism has its own style of butsudan, so craftsmen specialize in altars for a particular denomination. While some are of a relatively simple construction, others are extremely ornate, costing many thousands of dollars. Just as in the making of textiles in the Nishijin district, religious articles in the Honganji area are the product of a complicated division of labor, with every household contributing only a single part or step in the overall process. The tightly knit organization of communities that developed in Kyoto over the centuries owes a great deal to the interdependency of craftsmen such as these.

The objects sold in the Honganji district not only reflect religious concerns, but also the ornate aesthetic of the Momoyama Period, during which this area developed. In fact, a look at the Kara-mon gate of Nishi-Honganji, with its luxurious gold embellishments, leads one to believe that this may have set the tone for everything produced outside. The Kara-mon, or Chinese-style gate, is nicknamed the Higurashi mon...the "day-spending gate," implying that it takes a whole day to absorb all its beauties.

Incense and candles are two of the simpler articles of Buddhism to be found outside this elaborate gate. Incense is used in Japan for both religious purposes and for pleasure. Guessing the fragrance burned by the host was a popular Heian Period (794-1192) parlor game in the Imperial Court from which Kōdō, the incense ceremony still practiced today, evolved. The bright-red, top-heavy Buddhist candles are made of beeswax since the use of animal products such as tallow is against Buddhist philosophy. These candles are hand dipped in workshops throughout this neighborhood and their paper wicks burn with a tall, brilliant flicker.

56

There is irony in the fact that Kyoto's most notorious neighborhood lies just to the west of one of its most revered temples. Shimabara, the "nightless castle," as it has been called, is the name of the pleasure quarters behind Nishi-Honganji. The women of Shimabara were doomed to a life of prostitution within its walls when the Tokugawa Shogunate issued an edict in 1617 to confine such entertainment districts in order to control the merchant class that patronized them.

Sumi-ya, one of the last of the teahouses still standing in Shimabara, is a maze of rooms — one with hand-painted fans on the ceiling for the benefit of reclining guests, another with inlaid mother-of-pearl patterns in its midnight-blue walls. The famous woodblock-print artist Hokusai is said to have spent time dallying on the balconies of Sumi-ya during the Edo Period. This classic teahouse is recognized as a historic site and is undergoing restoration with the support of the government at this writing. Another teahouse, Wachigai-ya, is still in use and you may catch a glimpse of a geisha inside the huge noren curtain over the entrance.

A stroll through the Shimabara district leads you through its famous O-mon, the original gateway built in the 17th century beside which you will find a pyramid of buckets stacked, as they have been for centuries, in case of fire. The willow tree beside the O-mon gate has become a symbol of the transitory quality of life for which both Shimabara — and the Buddhist world — are famous.

57

54 The tiled roofs of Nishi-Honganji.

55 Though the gates of Higashi-Honganji.

56 The *karamon* gate, or Chinese-style gate, is nick-named the Higurashi-mon ... the "day-spending gate," implying that it takes a whole day to absorb all its beauties.

57 The *jinaichō*, or temple town, that lies between Nishi- and Higashi-Honganji temples.

58 Offerings before a *butsudan*, or Buddhist alter, in a Kyoto home.

59 The courtyard of Sumi-ya, a famous teahouse built in 1640 in the Shimabara district. The sumptuous interior, with its extravagantly painted screens and lacquered woodwork, still seems to echo with the voices of samurai revelers and their geisha women.

58

60

61

62

**60** The O-mon gateway to Shimabara, a reminde[r] the days when this entertainment district was closed within a wall. Guards kept watch at the g[ate] controlling the comings and goings of men — keeping the women virtual prisoners within.

**61** Once a year the last remaining *oiran*, the high[est] level of courtesan in the Edo Period, promen[ade] through the streets of Shimabara in their elabo[rate] finery.

**62** A 17th century woodblock print by Hiroshige de[pict]ing the one of gates to Shimabara.

**63** The entry to Sumi-ya, whose tightly gridded *kō[shi]mado* windows stretch for nearly a block in Shi[ma]bara.

## HONGANJI-SHIMABARA
(本願寺・島原)

**GETTING THERE:** Take City Bus No.5 from Sanjō Keihan Station and get off at "Higashi-Honganji-mae," or walk up Karasuma-dōri from Kyoto Station.

**SUGGESTED COURSE:**
❶ Higashi-Honganji → ❷ Honganji (jinai-chō) → ❸ Nishi-Honganji → ❹ Shimabara → ❺ O-mon Gate → ❻ Wachigai-ya → ❼ Sumi-ya

**FOR THE TAXI DRIVER:**
"東本願寺前まで行ってください。"
(Higashi-Honganji mae madé itte-kudasai.)
Please take me to the front of Higashi-Honganji.
(About ¥500 from the downtown area.)

**ESTIMATED TIME:** Three Hours.

### SUMI-YA

The teahouse known as Sumi-ya in Shimabara was designated as an Important Cultural Asset in 1952 in recognition of its historical and architectural significance as one of the finest extant examples of Edo Period (1603 – 1868) urban construction and design. It was the most luxurious of all such establishments in Kyoto during its heyday, and it became a gathering place for many famous men in the fields of art, literature, and politics, including *haiku* poet Yosa Buson, *ukiyo-e* artist Hiroshige, and political leader Ryoma Sakamoto.

43

# FUSHIMI
## ［伏見］

64

For the boatsmen who plied the rivers between Kyoto and Osaka in the 17th century, Fushimi was a stop to be remembered. More than a port town, Fushimi was the home of the finest saké makers in Japan, and so it remains today. No less than thirty-eight breweries still operate in this traditional neighborhood to the south of Kyoto, including Gekkeikan, the largest saké brewery in the world.

A twenty-minute ride from Sanjō Station on the Keihan Line takes you to Chūshojima. A short walk from the station leads you through the narrow little streets in this southern-most part of Fushimi to a willow-lined canal. Here you'll see the old saké warehouses in which Gekkeikan has been producing saké for the past three hundred years. The white walls and tiled roofs of these *saké kura*, as they are called, have become a symbol of this historic district.

Fushimi became the center of saké production over four centuries ago when Toyotomi Hideyoshi built his castle on a nearby hilltop, a place known as Fushimi Momoyama Castle. The rivers that converge here made Fushimi a natural port, linking it with the merchants of Sakai (now Osaka) in the south who could provide them with great quantities of the best rice available for saké-making. Pure water was another asset of Fushimi. The combination of castle, rivers, rice and water contributed to making Fushimi the saké capital of Japan. Walking the streets of Fushimi from Chūshojima, past the saké kura of Gekkeikan in the direction of Fushimi Momoyama Station, will take you through an old market district where you'll find shops selling everything from sushi to grilled quail — and all 38 brands of locally made saké.

Fushimi has a flavor all its own—a quality the Japanese call "robust." The latticed windows and doorways lack the fragile refinement of those in central Kyoto. Instead, they a sturdier, heavier, more permanent-looking than their counte parts farther north. Notice the decorative balconies on t second-floor windows of some of the homes that line t narrow side streets of Fushimi. Their curved balustrad reflect the architecture of the Momoyama Period (158 1600), because Fushimi was a *jōka-machi*, a town built at t foot of a castle, although only a replica of the original cast remains at Momoyama.

Terada-ya is another site of historic interest beside t canal at Chūshojima. This traditional inn or *ryokan* was t scene of a famous incident during the struggle to depose t Shogunate and restore the emperor to power in 1864. One the loyalists to the imperial court, a man named Sakamo Ryōma, now a folk hero very much in vogue with you students of history, once stayed at Terada-ya. The swo gouges that remain in the doorposts upstairs attest to t dramatic fight that ensued when Sakamoto's hideout w discovered by the Shogun's troops one night in 1864. Terad ya still operates as an inn, but opens its door daily to the ma history buffs who come to Fushimi to see it.

Taking the Keihan train one stop farther north to Fushir Inari leaves you a short walk down the road from Fushir Inari Taisha, the famous shrine to the goddess of rice. attracts hundreds of thousands of visitors each year, as it h since the eighth century. They come to pray for success business, as the orange *torii* gates that line the walk to the t of the hill attest. Each torii was donated by a mercha hoping to gain the blessings of Inari-san, as the shrine affectionately known to the people of Kyoto.

There are thousands of smaller branches of this shrine over the country that can be identified easily by the sm

66

stone foxes guarding their gates.

The steps up to the main shrine precincts are lined with shops selling religious objects, including charms and amulets, small natural-finish wood shrines, mirrors and ceramic Inari foxes...all important to the practice of Shinto. Note the gaily painted clay figurines sold in these shops. They are called *Fushimi ningyō*, or Fushimi dolls, and are perhaps the most popular souvenir of this district. They are purchased as good-luck charms, rather than toys, and represent heroic characters from old legends and myths. This type of clay doll is now produced in rural areas throughout Japan, but the prototypes are said to have come from Fushimi. The road running parallel with the train tracks at the foot of the shrine is a stretch of the old Tōkaido Highway system, the main thoroughfare during the 17th and 18th centuries.

67

**64** A *Fushimi ningyō*, the clay dolls sold as good-luck charms on the path that leads to the 1,200-year-old Fushimi Inari Jinja.

**65** A tunnel of orange *torii* donated by worshippers leads up the hillside behind Fushimi Inari, the shrine to the goddess of rice.

**66** The walls of the saké warehouses of Gekkeikan that line the canal in Fushimi.

**67** Special saké brewers called *tōji* travel from their homes in the countryside each winter to make saké for the thirty-eight saké companies in Fushimi. (Courtesy of Masuda Tokubei saké company.)

**68** Saké labels.

**69** Terada-ya, an inn in Fushimi where loyalist Saka-moto Ryōma fought with soldiers of the Shogunate during the uprising that restored the Emperor Meiji to power in 1864.

**68**

# FUSHIMI（伏見）

**GETTING THERE:** Take the Keihan train bound for Osaka from Sanjō Keihan Station and get off at Chūshojima (¥190). (Taxi fare would be exorbitant from the downtown area to Fushimi .)

**SUGGESTED COURSE:** ❶ Terada-ya → ❷ Gekkeikan Saké Warehouses and Museum＊→ ❸ Shopping Street → ❹ Abura-chō (Liquor Store) → ❺ Fushimi Momoyama Station (It is possible to walk up the hill to see the Momoyama Castle, but only a replica of the original remains) → ❻ Fushimi Inari → ❼ Fushimi Inari Taisha → ❽ The "tunnel" of orange torii gates

**ESTIMATED TIME:** Half a day.

＊Shown by appointment only. Ask at the TIC.

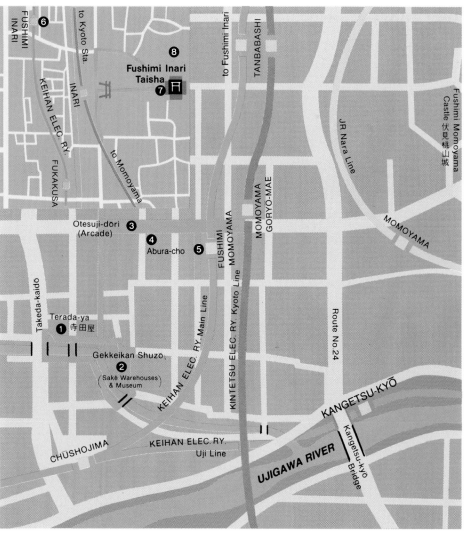

# LIFE IN THE MACHINAMI

*Water is essential to Kyoto. Rivers that feed, streams that purify, canals that carry... water that saves...kept in buckets beside doorways as a symbol of salvation from fire. Cooling, refreshing, restoring life.*

*The flow of life in the machinami of Kyoto encompasses a thousand years of trial and error...of flood and famine...of war and turmoil...of art and beauty. The culture that developed in these old neighborhoods was the foundation of life in Japan itself.*

*While they last, the machinami are symbols of a way of life that has taken centuries to evolve. The crafts that flourished here, the cuisine that simmered, the temples that arose, the shrines that inspired, the special touches that illuminated life, the tea ceremony... and so much more than these pages can hope to capture.*

*The twilight dim, the gentle breeze*
*By Nara-no-Ogawa stream*
*The splash of worshippers who wash*
*Before the shrine, all seem*
*A perfect summer's dream.*

*— Iyetaka Fujiwara (1237)*
*from Hyakunin Isshu*

# CRAFTS

*"Art is not a thing...
it is a way."*

A dimly lit tatami-mat room on a narrow alley in the heart of Kyoto...a craftsman sits on the floor of his workshop in front of a low wooden bench all day long...today, as he has done every day of his life since he was fifteen. His father worked at this same bench and the tools that hang on the walls around him have been handed down for generations. The patterns he follows are from the worn pages of a notebook that his grandfather kept nearly seventy years ago. This man makes wooden combs.

From the cutting of the tree to the final polish, it takes ten years to produce a single *tsuge-gushi*, or boxwood comb. Only the finest wood is used to make a comb that will become a family heirloom, passed down from grandmother to mother to daughter for years to come. The wood must be specially smoke-dried and cured for years before the craftsman cuts the piece from which the comb will be fashioned. He does not measure the teeth with a ruler — his hand and eye know the distance by heart.

The crafts of Kyoto are known for their refinement and elegance. Few objects made in Kyoto display the earthy, spontaneous flavor of folk crafts from the countryside. Instead, they reflect the studied precision and delicacy of an old established society, full of pride in its sometimes cumbersome traditions and customs, and its legacy as the classic imperial city of Japan.

Starting with the gift of techniques brought from China and Korea 1,200 years ago, the craftsmen who followed the Imperial Court to Kyoto in 794 began to mold and interpret these imported skills into a form of expression that was their own. They wrought an aesthetic that valued asymmetry and simplicity using techniques that allow the beauty of natural materials to be displayed to best advantage — understatement, subtlety and elegance in design. All this, combined with a color sense sometimes startling to the Western eye — a touch of bright green against a background of vermilion lacquer.

In the ten centuries Kyoto was the capital, it was the center for the production of the finest arts and crafts in Japan. Kyoto was not only the home of the Imperial Court, it was the center of religion, the scene of the development of aesthetic pursuits like the tea ceremony, and of the performing arts of music, theaters and dance. There were royal gar-

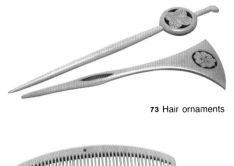

**73** Hair ornaments

**74** Combs

**75** A lacquered box

**76** Painted fans

**71** A combmaker cuts teeth in a boxwood comb — his hands 'remember' the space between.

**72** A woodblock print depicting a lacquerer's workshop in the Edo Period.

ments to be woven, serving trays to be lacquered, Buddhist statues to be carved and gilded, tea bowls to be thrown, iron kettles to be cast, musical instruments to be fashioned, and elaborate costumes to be designed, woven, embroidered, and dyed.

During the Muromachi Period (1334-1568), when craftsmanship was at its height in Kyoto, entire neighborhoods grew around a particular craft, like the weavers and dyers of Nishijin. The guilds they formed were under the protection of neighboring temples and shrines in whose precincts open markets were held, providing craftsmen with a stable income in return for tithings.

The relationship between families within a traditional neighborhood in Kyoto was tightly bound to the craft for which it was known. Each household undertook only one step in the process. A lacquerer only applied the lacquer to a wooden tray which someone else had made. Weavers did not dye their own thread, and dyers obtained their thread from someone else. In rural districts, this division of labor was not possible. Each farmer's family did everything themselves, from start to finish. The population in Kyoto, however, was large, and the finest craftsmen were attracted here to provide the Imperial Court and the feudal lords with finery.

Traces of the complicated system of guilds that developed over the centuries — and evidence of the high level of craftsmanship that was achieved — can still be found in the traditional craftsmen's workshops that remain in the old neighborhoods of Kyoto today.

**77**

**78**

**79**

**80**

**77** Noh mask carving

**78** Buddhist sculpture

**79** Tools of the trade are also handmade by Kyoto craftsmen.

**80** Basket weaving

**81** Pottery making

**82** Stone carving

**83** Gilding fabric

**84** Doll making

81

82

83

84

# CUISINE

An elegant banquet for a nobleman, a tea master's meticulous repast, the bare sustenance of a Zen priest, morsels to whet the appetite of a carousing samurai, simple fare for the working man ... *Kyo-ryōri*, or Kyoto cuisine, is an intriguing blend of a thousand years of history — and as many exotic ingredients — from fresh fern greens to bamboo shoots, from grilled river fish to pickled herring, from *yuba* to *fu*.

Yuba is perhaps the quintessential "Kyoto" ingredient. Skimmed from open vats of steaming soy milk, yuba is served fresh with a light sauce, or dried in strips or rolls (pictured on this page) to be used later in soups and a variety of inventive ways. Almost pure protein, yuba is an important ingredient in Zen vegetarian cooking (as is *fu*, its glutinous wheat counterpart). The flavor is subtle — indescribable; the texture delicate — thin as paper. Yuba is a backdrop against which other ingredients play — the blank space that defines the culinary lines. A master's touch to a cuisine that is truly an art.

The fusuma door slides open...s-s-s-h-u-s-h. A maid kneels outside...bows... apologizes quietly for the intrusion. You are seated on a pillow in a tatami room overlooking a garden...the sound of water trickling into a stone basin outside has helped to wash away the day's frustrations. You have been sitting here, sipping the green tea, eating the small sweet which has gently awakened your appetite...exactly as it was intended. The first lacquered tray of morsels appears just in time.

*Kaiseki* promises you'll never be bored. The meal you are served depends on the precise time of year. The best chefs guarantee their guests will never receive the same meal twice.

In Kyoto, a meal is to be savored by more than the palate. There is atmosphere in which to lavish, scenery to enjoy... there are gilt-edged bowls and inlaid-lacquer trays whose craftsmanship, design and color may also be imbibed... and aromas brought one at a time, to tantalize an appetite for the dish that follows. Kaiseki was designed to please emperors. It was refined and perfected by tea masters with a preference for simplicity and meticulous attention to the seasons. The Chinese characters (懐石) refer to the heated stones carried to bed inside the folds of the kimono of Zen monks... just enough to

86

ake the chill from their bellies. In the last centuries, kaiseki, written with different characters (会席), became hors d'oeuvres served with saké, for the merchant class out for a night of pleasure in the geisha houses of Gion. No matter what the occasion, Kyoto-style kaiseki places importance on seasonal ingredients, whose flavor is to be enhanced gently...never to be overwhelmed by heavy spices or elaborate sauces. It is intended to be served graciously, enjoyed leisurely, and appreciated attentively...like fine cuisine everywhere.

But Kyoto was more than aristocrats and playboys...the vast majority of people were farmers, shopkeepers and craftsmen who never got near a kaiseki meal. Kyoto was a landlocked city, a two-day trek over the mountains to the sea. Fish had to be salted or pickled to be carried that far on foot by peddlers. Even vegetables had to be pickled to save them from perishing in the hot, sticky summers. The people's cuisine of Kyoto was far from exotic. A bowl of barley rice, a few pickled vegetables, a bowl of miso soup — a bite of fish when times were good — and a cup of the plainest tea. Humble fare — often vegetarian, as much of the population was Buddhist.

*Shōjin-ryōri*, Zen-style cooking, served in temples and vegetarian restaurants today, turned the simple diet of Buddhist priests...vegetables, rice and soybeans... into a creative and interesting cuisine. Whatever is done in the life of a follower of Zen must be done with total attention and care. The cuisine that the painstaking monks evolved explored every imaginable use of its simple ingredients, especially of soybeans — a hundred ways to serve miso, soy sauce, tofu and yuba...all rich in protein. The same attention to visual beauty that other forms of Kyo-ryōri possess is found in shōjin-ryōri, though not to such a lavish degree. Nothing should be wasted, and rather than costly porcelain, the monks each had their own stack of lacquered bowls, one fitting inside the other...wiped clean by the monk himself when the meal had been thankfully consumed.

The dimensions of Kyo-ryōri, or Kyoto cuisine, reflect the seasons and sensibilities of all the townspeople — from priest to bon vivant, from nobility to peasant.

Today, a kaiseki meal can be extremely costly...but, an experience that needn't be missed. On a limited budget, a *Kaiseki bentō*, the "box lunch" supreme, will provide a delightful sampler of this magnificent cuisine.

85 *Yuba*, a Kyoto delicacy, skimmed from steaming soy milk, served in the soups and sauces of Kyoto cuisine.

86 *Yu-dofu*, simmered tofu to be dipped in soy sauce — one of the dishes featured in Zen vegetarian cooking.

87 *Kaiseki*, the classic Japanese meal — a treat for the eyes as well as the palate, and a specialty of Kyoto. (Courtesy of Kappo Yamashita restaurant.)

87

*Sabi*, the quiet dignity age alone can bestow — in the touch of blue-green patina time etches on bronze, in the yellowed borders of a paper scroll that has been unwrapped, admired, and put away safely a thousand times by a thousand careful hands. *Wabi*, the unpretentious beauty of an old ceramic bowl from the kilns of some anonymous country potter gone a hundred years —the humility poverty instills, a rustic simplicity...wild flowers, bamboo, water and stone. This is the spirit of *Sadō*, the tea ceremony: a simple bowl of tea, a meal shared with friends — thoughtfully, deliberately, savoring the moment in time.

The practice of ceremonial tea was originally brought to Japan from China, but the basic philosophy fit the Japanese people like a psychic glove. Perhaps that is why it is still so much alive in Japan today, when many other traditional cultural pursuits seem to have worn thin with time.

The tea ceremony has left its mark on almost every aspect of life in Japan from arts and crafts to cuisine, from social customs to psychology. The impact of Sadō is everywhere to be found —in the way houses were built, in the food people eat, even in relationships between friends — and nowhere more so than in the old neighborhoods of Kyoto.

Though Sadō was originally a pastime enjoyed exclusively by members of the aristocracy, it was the merchant class, with its aspirations to rival the upper classes, that eventually brought the aesthetics of the tea ceremony into the mainstream of Japanese society in the 17th and 18th centuries.

Few of the traditional merchant homes of Kyoto are without a formal tea room, based on the original four-and-a-half tatami-mat tea room built in the 15th century by Shogun Ashikaga Yoshimasa at his villa now known as Ginkakuji, the Temple of the Silver Pavilion. This tea room became the standard, not only for

# TEA CEREMONY

**88**

other tea rooms, but for Japanese architecture as a whole from then on.

The proportions, the natural materials, the use of light and shadow are all aesthetic considerations inspired by the tea ceremony. The *zashiki*, the formal guest room of a traditional home always had a special alcove in which a hanging scroll, a flower arrangement, and perhaps a treasured family possession were placed.

Not only interior but exterior features of homes in Kyoto show the influence of tea. Even the smallest *machiya* had an interior garden, though some consist of but a few carefully placed rocks, a stand of bamboo, and a stone water basin in an open-air niche the size of a hall closet. The *tsubo-niwa*, a special feature of the machiya of Kyoto, are often no bigger than a large ceramic crock (*tsubo*). As in the classic tea room, no home is without a touch of nature, however small, even in the midst of a crowded city.

Entering the home of a prosperous merchant family to find two or perhaps three exquisite gardens tucked within its recesses away from public view is a delightful prospect. The somber, heavily slatted façades of these homes conceal the wealth and tastes of their owners from ordinary passers-by. In poorer neighborhoods, areas that once housed the servants and employees of wealthy merchants, the presence of nature can be seen in the carefully tended shelves laden with potted chrysanthemums, morning glories and bonsai clinging to the very edge of the street. The flowers displayed outside these modest dwellings announce the changing seasons. Every miniature pine and azalea is snipped and trimmed with the care, patience and dedication even a tea master would admire.

**89**

**88** A tea room built in accordance with an aesthetic of simplicity and natural beauty.

**89** This *tsubo-niwa* adds the smallest touch of nature to a traditional Kyoto home — a feature influenced by the tea ceremony.

**90** The tea ceremony — minimalism, balance and composure.

# FESTIVALS

Small, white-faced boy, teeth blackened, lips scarlet, robed in costly brocade, crowned with a golden phoenix, will ride this year — as he has since the tenth century — from Yasaka Jinja through the streets of Kyoto to perform a spiritual rite in the name of the common people. He is the *chigo*, the boy chosen this year from among the merchant families of central Kyoto as a messenger of Susano-o, the Shinto god to whom this magical festival, Gion Matsuri, is dedicated.

The chigo has been preparing for this task for an entire year —training in the complicated rituals he will need to perform. After weeks of special purification ceremonies, during which he lives in pampered isolation from contaminating influences (such as the presence of women...), the chigo is carried atop the lead float, the *naginata*, where he must cut the rope that marks the start of the procession on July 17th. Failure to sever the rope with one stroke of the sword is a dishonor to his family name forever — such responsibility for a child of ten.

92

Gion Matsuri has always belonged to the people. It originated in a plea to the gods to stop a plague which swept the ancient capital in the ninth century. Sixty-six halberds representing the sixty-six provinces of old Japan were offered by the Emperor Seiwa to appease the angry gods who were thought to have inflicted the disastrous epidemic. When the plague miraculously abated, it was decreed that a procession be held annually in thanksgiving — and to ensure that no such horror would ever again befall the city. This festival is conducted under the auspices of Yasaka Jinja, or Gion-sha, as the shrine is locally known because of its location in the heart of the Gion district.

Over the turbulent centuries of civil war that marked the middle ages in Japan, the citizens themselves took on the responsibility for the festival. By the Edo Period (1603-1868) the rising merchant class had begun to use the festival as a means of asserting their newly gained wealth and power in a feudalistic society which had relegated them to the lowest ranks. The floats, called *yama* and *hoko*, were adorned with the finest tapestries and treasures, some of which were obtained from European traders with whom the merchants of Kyoto conducted their

91

prosperous ventures.

Although World War II brought a temporary halt to the festival, it was soon afterward revived, and today it stands as one of the largest and most beloved festivals in the country. Several of the smaller floats which were lost or damaged over the centuries have been restored in recent years, and the weavers of the Nishijin area continue to offer the finest new tapestries to replace those that have been destroyed. Kept in special storehouses dotted throughout the central merchant district of Kyoto, the floats and their priceless regalia remain in the care of the townspeople today.

The cultural significance of Gion Matsuri, particularly to the people of Kyoto, lies not only in the festival's historical continuity, but also in its expression of the irrepressible nature of the common people. Throughout feudal times and amidst a rigidly structured class system, Gion Matsuri was always a rallying point for the populace of Kyoto.

Today, visitors from all over the world come to watch the July 17th procession and marvel at the splendor of the thirty-one floats as they pass by, one after another, their giant wooden wheels now facing asphalt pavement — their halberds challenging power lines on high.

*Matsuri*, the word for festival in Japanese, comes from the word *matsuru*, which means to offer prayer. Gion

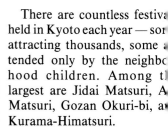

Matsuri, like most of the other festivals in Japan, has its roots in religion. It is one of the *goryō-e* festivals, which originated as a means of appeasing the gods who were thought to cause fires, floods and earthquakes if not sufficiently placated by the citizens of Kyoto.

There are over 2,000 shrines and temples in Kyoto, each one an integral part of the life of the neighborhood in which it stands. The people are responsible for the care of their local shrine, and it is they who carry on its traditional ceremonies and festivals.

There are countless festiva[l]s held in Kyoto each year — so[me] attracting thousands, some [at]tended only by the neighbo[r]hood children. Among t[he] largest are Jidai Matsuri, A[oi] Matsuri, Gozan Okuri-bi, a[nd] Kurama-Himatsuri.

The smallest of all—Jizōb[on] —is a summer festival in hon[or] of the Buddhist deity Jiz[ō,] special guardian of childre[n.] During Jizōbon, people dec[o]rate a little shrine to Jizō in eve[ry] Kyoto neighborhood, and th[e] children carry the portab[le] shrine through the streets to p[ay] homage. These shrines are ten[d]ed year-round by the women [of] every neighborhood, each [of] whom takes a turn cleaning a[nd] placing flowers there, a custo[m] that is still observed toda[y.] Once a year in the midst of t[he] heat of August, the little on[es] gather for Jizōbon to play gam[es] and vie for prized plastic baub[les] on mats spread out in front [of] the neighborhood shrine, while their gran[d]parents look on dotingly and sip co[ld] barley tea. Of all the grand festivals cel[e]brated in this old city, the importance [of] religion as a focal point for communi[ty] spirit in the traditional neighborhoods [of] Kyoto can be seen most clearly in simp[le] neighborhood festivals like these.

**91** The *chigo* of Gion Matsuri, a ten-year-old messe[n]ger of the gods, preparing to cut the rope that sta[rts] this thousand-year-old festival.

**92** Lanterns on the floats of Gion Matsuri.

**93** *Gozan-Okuribi* — Chinese characters are burned [on] the mountainsides each year to light the way for [the] return of ancestral spirits to the heavens.

**94** Aoi Matsuri

**95** Kurama Himatsuri

**96** Jidai Matsuri

94

95

96

# SHRINES
# AND
# TEMPLES

*Don...don...don...*you have to listen more carefully now than in days gone by. The roar of the traffic drowns it out unless you pay attention. Once at dawn...again at dusk, the sonorous bronze temple bells of Kyoto still ring every day. *Clap...clap...*the women stop for a moment of prayer on their way to do the shopping, clapping twice before the neighborhood shrine.

Buddhism and Shintoism live side by side in Kyoto. They demand little of its citizens these days, though each had their turn at power and glory. You are taken to a Shinto shrine when you are born, to a Buddhist temple when you die...in between you observe the customs, festivals and ceremonies of both...respectfully, but not always "religiously," in a Western sense. Though some are true devotees to particular sects, the majority of people in Kyoto adopt a "why take chances" attitude about religion. You pray to the gods when you're in trouble, you thank them for favors when you remember...when you get old, you take it all much more seriously. Two thousand shrines and temples exist in Kyoto, and none appear neglected.

There are the famous temples of Zen — Nanzen-ji, Daitoku-ji, Ryōan-ji, Tenryū-ji, Myōshin-ji — famous for their contemplative rock gardens and brush paintings; the older, more esoteric hallows—Enryaku-ji, Tō-ji, Sanjusangen-dō, with their complicated mysticism and Byzantine practices. Many famous temples were former villas — Kinkaku-ji, Ginkaku-ji and Tenryū-ji. The oldest and most beloved temple of all in Kyoto is Kiyomizu-dera, perched upon the side of a hill in eastern Kyoto since the 8th century.

Some of Japan's most beloved shrines stand in Kyoto, behind their bright orange *torii* gates — Fushimi Inari, Yasaka Jinja, Kitano Jinja, Heian Jingū. The pair of Kamigamo and Shimogamo Jinja predate the arrival of the Emperor Kanmu and his court to this valley in the eighth century.

The temples honor the teachings of Buddha brought from China in the sixth century. The shrines honor ancestral spirits and a host of indigenous gods of nature — fire, thunder, water, rain, fertility, and more. Their approach to each other is one of tolerance — their philosophies harmonize more than they conflict.

For the townspeople of Kyoto, both the shrines and the temples are central to the life of every community, economically as well as spiritually. Throngs of pilgrims travel from all parts of the country to visit the great religious centers of Kyoto, each needing food and lodging, and hoping to bring back a string of prayer beads, some incense, or a home altar as a blessed memento of their journey — all providing income to the craftsmen and shopkeepers outside the temple gates.

During the middle ages, many of the shrines and temples opened their gates to the merchants of Kyoto, in exchange for tithes, providing a safe place to sell their wares during unstable times. The flea markets held today at Tō-ji on the 21st of every month, and at Kitano Jinja on the 25th have been there for centuries.

The merchant's guilds that formed in the fourteenth century each paid homage (and money) to the particular shrine that housed their guardian spirit. Kitano Jinja was patronized by saké makers, cotto merchants worshipped at Yasaka Jin ...there was a patron shrine for ever occupation from fishmonger to Kabu actor...and so it is today.

Here a small stone Jizō stands, e shrined beneath a small wooden roof. H is the guardian deity of children an around his neck hangs a little bib...plac here in prayer and sorrow by a moth who has lost her child. There an old ma climbs slowly all the way up Daimonji pray at the small stone shrines along t steep path. At the mountain spring th flows at Kiyomizu-dera, a devotee chan a shivery sutra as the icy water flows ov his head at dawn on a winter morning. T gods are not neglected in Kyoto.

**97** The main hall of Tō-ji temple, erected in 1380.
**98** The vermilion walls of Yasaka Shrine.
**99** The monthly flea market at Tō-ji.
**100** A neighborhood shrine to the Buddhist deity a guardian of children, Jizō.

# INFORMATION

## GLOSSARY

**yu** — a small, white river fish (a delicacy in Kyoto)

**engara-gōshi** — a rust-colored latticework (gōshi) that covers the windows of some types of homes in Kyoto

**ento** — a box lunch

**unkazai** — cultural asset or treasure

**utsudan** — a Buddhist home altar

**higo** — the child who represents the gods and rides in the lead float of Gion Matsuri

**hō** — a township

**-)chōnai** — 'inside' a township; a term that defines a community and its affairs within a township

**hōnaikai** — the community organization to which members of a cho belong

**aidokoro** — the kitchen; the utility space

**anna** — lord; master; husband; patron

**—** glutinous wheat cake (a delicacy in Kyoto)

**ushimi ningyō** — clay dolls from Fushimi

**usuma** — opaque sliding paper doors

**eiko** — Kyoto dialect for geisha

**onin-gumi** — the smallest social unit within a Kyoto neighborhood; five families who are mutually responsible for each other's actions

**oryō-e** — festivals held to appease gods who were thought to cause natural disasters (e.g, Gion Matsuri)

**ata** — weaver's loom; the name of a Chinese family who immigrated to Kyoto and taught the Japanese how to weave

**uyarai** — lit. 'dog barrier'; a bamboo barrier to shield the front of a house from dogs and other intruders

**haichō** — a township within the precincts of a temple

**nja/jingū** — a shrine

**ka-machi** — a township built at the foot of a castle

**aiseki-ryōri** — formal Japanese cuisine served in several courses

**amado** — old-style wood-burning clay stoves

**mi** — spirit; god

**mi-dana** — lit. 'spirit shelf'; a home shrine dedicated to Shinto gods

**yomizu-yaki** — ceramics from the Kiyomizu district

**idō** — the incense ceremony; a custom which evolved from court games in which guests tried guess the fragrance their host burned for them

**mayose** — a wooden rail in front of some Kyoto homes formerly used as a hitching post for horses

**ishi** — a wooden latticework that covers the windows of homes in Kyoto, used for privacy

**ura** — a storehouse; a treasure house

**yo-ryōri** — Kyoto cuisine

**machinami** — lit. 'city rows'; refers to a line of city rowhouses

**machiya** — city house

**maiko** — an apprentice geisha

**matsuri (matsuru)** — festival (to pray)

**mingei** — folk art

**misenoma** — shop room; usually the room closest to the street in a Kyoto merchant's house

**mizuya** — a kitchen cabinet for storing dried goods and utensils

**monzenchō** — a township formed at the gate of a temple

**naginata** — the first float in the Gion Matsuri procession

**nakaniwa** — the central garden of a Kyoto home

**Nishijin-ori** — textiles woven in Nishijin

**noren** — doorway curtain, often bearing the family crest and hung out to indicate that the shop is open for business

**obi** — a kimono sash

**o-chaya** — lit. a 'teahouse'; refers to houses in the entertainment districts at which geisha entertained their guests

**pokkori geta** — the high-platformed wooden shoes worn by apprentice geisha

**sadō** — the tea ceremony

**saké kura** — a saké warehouse

**sashimi** — slices of raw fish served with soy sauce and wasabi condiments

**senbon-gōshi** — lit. 'thousand-fingered lattices'; refers to very closely arranged slats that cover windows in parts of Kyoto

**shaké-machi** — a township of the families of shrine priests

**shamisen** — a three-stringed musical instrument

**shinko dango** — round rice cakes served at shops at the foot of Atago Jinja in western Kyoto

**shōjin-ryōri** — Zen-style vegetarian cuisine

**tatami** — straw mats used as flooring in traditional Japanese homes

**tera/ji** — a temple

**tokonoma** — the alcove of the formal guest room or tea room of a Japanese house

**torii** — the gate of a Shinto shrine

**tōriniwa** — the long breezeway that runs the length of a Kyoto house

**tsuge-gushi** — a boxwood comb

**tsukemono** — Japanese-style pickles

**tsuzure-ori** — figured brocade (also known as 'fingernail weaving')

**ukiyo-e** — woodblock prints depicting the 'floating world', the world of entertainment and pleasure

**unagi no nedoko** — lit. the 'bedrooms of eels'; refers to the long narrow Kyoto-style houses

**yama/hoko** — two types of elaborately decorated floats that participate in the procession during Gion Matsuri

**yoshi** — a type of reed used to thatch the roofs of homes in rural parts of Japan

**yuba** — soy milk skimmings, a Kyoto delicacy

**yūzen** — wax-resist dyeing developed in Kyoto by a 17th-century artist named Miyasaki Yūzen

**wasabi** — a condiment similar to horseradish served with raw fish

**zashiki** — the formal guest room of a Japanese house

## THE KYOTO TOURIST INFORMATION CENTER

The number of tours, museums, galleries, workshops, temples, gardens, shops and restaurants in Kyoto is enough to keep you (and the authors of guidebooks) busy for years. The fastest way to get the particular information you need is to call (☎371-0480 or 371-5649), or better yet visit the Kyoto TIC (Tourist Information Center) at their office on the ground floor of the Kyoto Tower Building on Karasuma-dōri in front of Kyoto Station. (Open from 9 a.m. to 5 p.m., Monday through Friday; from 9 a.m. to noon on Saturdays). No matter what you are interested in seeing, studying, tasting, visiting or watching (within reason, please) you can get help in both English and French at the TIC. (Ask about their volunteer guide service.)

## TRANSPORTATION

Kyoto has six bus lines, five trains, one subway, and more cabs than any other city in Japan. Because of the unpredictability of signs or instructions in English, it is often wisest to call the TIC for information on the fastest, most economical way to get where you want to go. Maps are also available free of charge at the TIC.

Taxis are a reliable and timesaving alternative for those with a limited schedule. (Flag drops at ¥420 for the first 2 km; ¥80 per 540 m thereafter — not unreasonably priced, particularly if shared.)

Try Kyoren Taxi Company (☎075-221-1210) or MK Taxi Company (☎075-721-2237), both of which offer service in English, including tours with English-speaking guides.

Bicycle rentals are available, but traffic is hectic on most of the main streets.

Using the centrally located Sanjō Keihan bus and train station beside the Kamogawa River in the downtown area as a starting point, basic bus information and directions for cab drivers in Japanese have been provided under each of the different historic neighborhood sections in this book. Once you have arrived in the vicinity, see these areas on foot. One very important thing to remember is YOUR FEET. Wear comfortable, well-broken-in shoes, and DON'T FORGET that in most Japanese restaurants, homes, and inns you will have to take them off. Hence, the popularity of slip-on shoes in Japan.

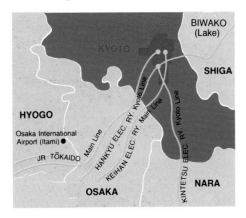

## ENGLISH LANGUAGE BOOKSTORES

For maps, guidebooks and books in English on everything from making sushi to collecting swords, visit Maruzen Bookstore on Kawara-machi Street between Shijō and Sanjō, or Izumiya Bookstore in the Avanti Building south of Kyoto Station. Look for monthly magazines like the *Kansai Time Out* or the *Kyoto Journal* for up-to-date information on local exhibitions, festivals and other cultural events. Two free tourist publications, the *Kyoto Monthly Guide* and the *Kyoto Visitors' Guide,* are available at the TIC and at most of the major hotels.

*OLD KYOTO, A Guide to Traditional Shops, Restaurants, and Inns,* Diane Durston's first book, was published in 1986 by Kodansha International. It not only leads visitors through the backstreets to explore the old shops, out-of-the-way restaurants, and traditional ryokan, but tells the stories of the shopkeepers themselves, providing a personal glimpse of Kyoto as a way of life that has lasted 1,200 years. At bookstores throughout Japan for ¥1,800 (U.S. $11.95).

## ACKNOWLEDGMENTS

This book is the product of the efforts of many people in Kyoto who are sincerely interested in preserving what remains of the historic neighborhoods of Kyoto and the traditions they have given shelter to for so many centuries. I would like to thank the Director of the Kyoto City Planning Bureau, Mr. Hiroo Kinoshita, for giving his valuable time to assist my research; Mr. Mitsuhiro Nishiguchi, the City Manager of Traditional Arts and Crafts; Mr. Wataru Morimoto, the Manager of the Kyoto Dentō Sangyō Kaikan; Mr. Susumu Hatano, the Senior Director of the Information Department of Kyoto Shinkin Bank; Mr. Keiji Fujimoto, the Deputy Secretary General of the Kyoto Association of Corporate Executives; Mr. Zenzaburo Yamamori, the Director of the Kyoto Tourist Bureau; and Mr. Hironobu Takuma, of the Kyoto International Conference Hall, for their support of this project.

And thank you, once again, to Professor Yasuo Kitazawa, for encouragement, advice, and for sharing an Osakan's hard-won Kyoto know-how.

I would also like to thank French architect Claire Gallian, who has been studying the history of Japanese architecture for the past seven years at Kyoto University. Her research on minka and machiya in the Kyoto area has made a valuable contribution to preservationist efforts in Japan. Without her generous assistance this book would not have been possible.

Thank you, also, to the fine group of Kyoto photographers who have spent much of their energies preserving this city on film for us all: Kenzo Yamamoto, Katsuhiko Mizuno, Hiroko Matsuo, and Toshio Honda. Thank you to Lucy Birmingham whose visual sensibilities always fill in the gaps left behind by my words. And to Shuji Toda, a designer who has shown patience beyond the call of duty.

Thank you to Joseph Cronin, for trying to mend the holes in my fences and straighten my literary tie, and to Mikiko Murata, whose faith keeps me going.

Finally, to my publisher, Mr. Kinzo Honda and the entire staff of Mitsumura Suiko Shoin, who have trusted, cooperated with, encouraged, and coddled this gaijin writer from beginning to end...thank you so very much. Particularly to Mr. Hirosato Ono, my editor, who lost lots of sleep, gave up weekends, worked long into the night, and did his very best to understand the thoughts behind my clumsy Japanese words...thank you.

### PHOTO CREDITS

Kenzo Yamamoto
10, 13, 18, 26, 27, 31, 32, 34, 35, 50, 59, 63, 90, 92, 93, 95, 97, 98

Katsuhiko Mizuno
2, 6, 7, 9, 14, 15, 16, 19, 21, 23, 24, 25, 28, 29, 30, 33, 36, 37, 38, 39, 43, 44, 45, 46, 52, 55, 60, 61, 64, 65, 66, 67, 68, 69, 70, 84, 85, 86, 87, 88, 89, 91, 94, 96, 100

Hiroko Matsuo
20, 41, 42, 47, 48, 49, 51

Toshio Honda
3, 4, 5, 8, 11, 12, 17, 22, 54, 56, 58, 73, 74, 76, 99

Lucy Birmingham
71

Traditional Craft Section, Commerce and Industry Division, Economic Affairs Bureau of Kyoto City Government
75, 78, 79, 80, 82, 83

Kyoto Dentō Sangyō Kaikan (Museum of Traditional Industry)
57, 77, 81

Kyoto Sōgo Shiryō-kan (Kyoto Library Museum)
I-4, 40, 62, 72

Hayashibara Museum
1

### ILLUSTRATIONS

Susumu Hatano
I-8

City Planning Bureau of Kyoto City Government
I-1, I-3, I-5, I-6, I-7

Reprinted from (WINDS) magazine
I-2

### MAPS

Plus Alpha

# KYOTO

☐ : The seven historic districts are
indicated by boxes.

1. Sanneizaka district.
2. Gion Shinbashi district.
3. Sagano Toriimoto district.
4. Kamigamo Shake-machi district.
5. Nishijin district.
6. Honganji/Shimabara district.
7. Fushimi district.

to Kurama

Kamigamo Jinja
Ota Jinja
Azekura

4

KAMO GAWA RIVER

Kitayama-dōri

Kyoto Prefectural Library

The Prefectural Botanical Garden

Imamiya Jinja

Daisen-in

Daitoku-ji

KITAŌJI
Kitaōji-dōri

Kinkaku-ji

KURAMAGUCHI

Shimogamo Jinja

Kyoto Prince Hotel

Ryōan-ji
Ritsumeikan Univ.

Shōkoku-ji

Kyoto American Center

DEMACHI-YANAGI

Hirano Jinja

Ninna-ji

RYŌAN-JI-MICHI

Tōji-in

Kitano Jinja

5

Dōshisha Univ.

IMADEGAWA

Imadega

TAKAOGUCHI

OMURO MYŌSHINJI

TŌJI-IN

KITANO-HAKUBAICHŌ

Nishijin Textile Center

Karasuma-dōri

SUBWAY Karasuma Line

Kyoto Imperial Palace

NARUTAKI

Myōshin-ji

Kyoto Prefectural Government

Kyoto Palaceside Hotel

Kawaramachi-dōri

KAMO GAWA RIVER

Higashiōji-dōri

TOKIWA

to Sagano

HANAZONO

JR SAN'IN Main Line

Hotel New Kyoto

Marutamachi-dōri

MARUTAMACHI

to Kameoka

Uzumasa Eigamura

Nijō Castle

Kyoto Chamber of Commerce & Industry

Hotel Fujita Kyoto

to Arashiyama

KATABIRA NO TSUJI

UZUMASA

KAIKONO-YASHIRO

Nishiōji-dōri

Senbon-dōri

International Hotel Kyoto

Kyoto ANA Hotel

Horikawa-dōri

Kyoto Hotel

Kyoto City Government

Kyoto Municipal Museum of Traditional Ind

NIJŌ

Oike-dōri

OIKE

Hiiragiya-Inn

Kyoto Royal Hotel

KEIFUKU Arashiyama Line

YAMANOUCHI

SANJŌGUCHI

Sanjō-dōri

Hotel Gimmond Kyoto

Tawaraya-Inn
Sumiya-Inn

SANJŌ

SANJŌ

2

SAIIN

SHIJŌ OMIYA

Shijō-dōri

KARASUMA

Daimaru Dept. Store

KAWARAMACHI

SHIJŌ

Kyoto Cr

SAI

SHIJŌ OMIYA

Karasuma Kyoto Hotel

SHIJŌ

Takashimaya Dept. Store

Hankyu Dept. Store

KDD

Gion Hotel

Yasa

TENJIN GAWA RIVER

Kennin-ji

Nishikyogoku Sports Center

NISHI KYŌGOKU

Omiya-dōri

Gojō-dōri

GOJŌ

6

KEIHAN ELEC. R.Y.

GOJŌ

Ro

Kyoto Tōkyū Hotel

TANBA-GUCHI

Route No. 9

HANKYU ELEC. R.Y. Kyoto Line

Nishi-Honganji

Higashi-Honganji

Kyoto National

Shichijō-dōri

Hotel New Hankyu Kyoto

Kintetsu Dept. Store

SHICHIJŌ

Kyoto Park Hotel

KATSURA GAWA RIVER

Kyoto Grand Hotel

Kyoto Tower Hotel

Kyoto Century Hotel

Sanjusagendō

to Arashiyama

Katsura Imperial Villa

Steam Locomotive Museum

JR KYOTO STA.

Hotel Keihan Kyoto

JR SHINKAN

KATSURA

NISHIOJI

Hachijō-dōri

New Miyako Hotel

TŌFUKUJI

to Umeda

to Shin-Osaka

Tō-ji

TŌJI

Kujō-dōri

to Fushimi

to Fushimi

Tōfuku-ji

to Osaka

# SAGANO
to Mt. Atago

TAKARAGAIKE

Adashino Nenbutsu-ji
Daikaku-ji
Osawa pond
Hirosawa pond
Giō-ji
Nison-in
Saga Syakadō
Enri-an
Hōkyō-in
Takiguchi-dera
Jōjakkō-ji
Rakushisha
Shin Marutamachi-dōri
SAGA
Shūgakuin Imperial Villa
SHŪGAKUIN
JR SAN'IN Main Line
to Kyoto Sta.
Rokuō-in
KEIFUKU ARASHIYAMA Line
Tenryū-ji
SAGAEKI-MAE
ROKUŌ-IN
KURUMA-ZAKI
ARASHIYAMA
ARISUGAWA
KATABIRANO-TSUJI
Shisendō
OI GAWA RIVER
KATSURA GAWA RIVER
ARISU GAWA RIVER
Hōrin-ji
ARASHI-YAMA
Shijō-dōri
MATSUO
Matsuo Taisha
HANKYU ELEC. RY. Arashiyama Line
Ginkaku-ji
Shirakawa-dōri
Saihō-ji (Koke-dera)
KAMI-KATSURA
Route No. 9
to Kawara-machi
KATSURA
Hotel Sunflower Kyoto
Nomura Museum
Nanzen-ji
AGE

# FUSHIMI
TŌJI
Kujō-dōri
JŪJŌ
Jūjō-dōri
TOBAKAIDŌ
Mt. Inari
FUSHIMI INARI
Fushimi Inari Taisha
KINTETSU ELEC. RY.
KAMO GAWA RIVER
INARI
KAMI-TOBAGUCHI
FUKAKUSA
Route No. 24
FUJINOMORI
Meishin Expressway
Kyoto Minami I.C.
KEIHAN ELEC. RY.
KUJŌYAMA
TAKEDA
Jōnan-gū
SUMIZOME
to Hamaōtsu
FUSHIMI
HINOOKA
Kyoto Trade Fair Center
JR NARA Line
MISASAGI
KATSURA GAWA RIVER
Route No. 1
TANBABASHI
TANBA-BASHI
Fushimi Momoyama Castle
MOMOYAMA GORYOMAE
Kyoto Tōkyū Inn
FUSHIMI MOMOYAMA
MOMOYAMA
to Tokyo
KANGETSU-KYŌ
MOMOYAMA MINAMIGUCHI
CHŪSHOJIMA
UJI GAWA RIVER
to Kyobashi

# LOCATION

VLADIVOSTOK
SAPPORO
PEKING
PYONGYANG
SEOUL
KYOTO
TOKYO
SHANGHAI
FUKUOKA
OSAKA
TAIPEI

45°
40°
35°
30°
25°
120° 125° 130° 135° 140°

# URBAN SIZE

## BOSTON
Population (City Area)
562,994 (1980)

Urbanized Area
City Area
Main Road

## KYOTO
Population (City Area)
1,473,065 (1980)

# URBAN HISTORY

Urbanized Area
Old Imperial Palace
Main Street
River

Original plan of street (The Heian era (794~))

Present

The Muromachi Era (1338–1573)

# KYOTO IS A HISTORICAL CITY

A.D. 2000 1500 1000 500 0 B.C. 500

ROME (B.C. 753)
SIAM 582
KYOTO (B.C. 1100)
KÖLN 794
PARIS 795
LONDON 987
NEW YORK 1066
TOKYO 1590
BOSTON 1625
1630

I-8